THE VINEGAR TREE

THE
VINEGAR TREE

A Play

by

PAUL OSBORN

FARRAR & RINEHART, *Incorporated*
On Murray Hill NEW YORK

PS 3529
.S15
V5
1931x

TO TOM

The following is a copy of the program of the first performance of THE VINEGAR TREE, at The Playhouse, New York City, Wednesday evening, November 19th, 1930:

DWIGHT DEERE WIMAN

PRESENTS

MARY BOLAND

in

THE VINEGAR TREE

by Paul Osborn

Directed by Winchell Smith
Settings by Raymond Sovey

CAST

(In order of appearance)

MAX LAWRENCE	Warren William
AUGUSTUS MERRICK	H. Reeves-Smith
WINIFRED MANSFIELD	Katherine Wilson
LOUIS	Walter Colligan
LAURA MERRICK	Mary Boland
LEONE MERRICK	Helen Brooks
GEOFFRY COLE	Allen Vincent

SCENES

Act One

Living room of the Merrick's country house. Late afternoon.

Act Two

Same. After dinner.

Act Three

The porch. 3 A.M.

THE VINEGAR TREE

ACT ONE

ACT I

SCENE: *The living room of the Merrick's country house. Door at left into hall; French windows at back, right and left, opening onto a large porch upon which is seen wicker furniture. The porch and grounds beyond are quite visible through the windows when they are open. At present, since it is late afternoon of a day in early summer, the porch and grounds are bathed in mellow sunlight and are lighter than the room itself.*

AUGUSTUS, an old man of sixty, is seated on the porch near the open window at left. He is sleeping over an open book. MAX, who looks about forty, is standing near the window gazing down at him. He has a pad and pencil with which he is making a sketch. Now and then he stops, studies AUGUSTUS more closely, steps back for a different angle or better light and then continues his sketch. On the floor by the hall door is a traveling bag and a large canvas bag commonly used by painters to carry the ungainly implements of their craft.

A few moments elapse. MAX looks at his watch impatiently, listens for a moment, rings, listens again, shakes his head and with a shrug continues

[3]

his sketch. The silence and dusk cause a feeling of solitude to pervade the room. Occasionally AUGUSTUS *snores.*

Suddenly WINIFRED *is heard calling in the hall. She is a handsome lady of about thirty-five, dressed in smart tailored-suit and carrying a traveling bag. As she calls,* MAX *turns to the hall, startled. Then he goes quickly to the window near* AUGUSTUS *and closes it cautiously, with an apprehensive "Oh, Lord!" He is closing it as* WINIFRED *enters.*

WINIFRED

[In the hall.]
Laura! Augustus! Where the devil is everybody? What's the matter with the doorbell? Isn't there anyone to bring in my luggage? Aren't you expecting me? Is this a morgue? Damn! Laura!
[She enters.]

MAX

[At the window, in a loud whisper.]
Winifred!

WINIFRED

[Gaily.]
Max, darling! You beat me after all! I'm delighted.
[She starts for him with open arms.]

MAX

[Pointing to AUGUSTUS.*]*
Shh! For Heaven's sakes! That's charming of you,

[4]

of course. But please be delighted without mention-
ing any names.

WINIFRED

[*Stopping short.*]
Oh! I didn't see anyone there. I thought the place
was deserted.

MAX

[*At window seeing if* AUGUSTUS *was wakened.*]
No place is ever deserted. That's the first lesson in
discretion. The second is never to enter a room shout-
ing "Max, darling."

WINIFRED

Oh, don't be instructive! Did he hear me?

MAX

[*With another look at* AUGUSTUS]
I guess not. He's evidently dead.

WINIFRED

[*Going to him.*]
Fine. Then that's all right.
[*She throws her arms around his neck.*]
How are you, sweet?
[*They embrace.*]

MAX

Scared to death. Look here, Winifred, your coming
in right now makes the situation damned awkward.

WINIFRED

What's the matter? Still afraid they're going to find out about us?

MAX

More afraid than ever. What do you say to jumping in the car and going right back to the city?

WINIFRED

Now don't start that again, Max. I've got you down here and we're going to stay. Oh, we're going to have a beautiful week. Listen.

[*Silence.*]

Isn't it heavenly? Isn't it a relief from that hot studio of yours?

MAX

Of course it is. But this country air is going to make you fearfully indiscreet. That's the trouble with you women who have amiable husbands. You never have any skill in deception.

WINIFRED

Nonsense! I can be as deceitful as you!

MAX

But you don't realize the position we're in.

WINIFRED

Don't I! It's my favorite position.

[6]

MAX

[*Freeing himself.*]
Oh, Lord. Let go! He might wake up.

WINIFRED

[*Laughing.*]
Who is he anyway?

MAX

How should I know? Don't you?

WINIFRED

[*Peering at* AUGUSTUS.]
Why— It might be— I believe it *is!* It *must*
be! It's Gussy himself! Doesn't he look ferocious?

MAX

And who's Gussy?

WINIFRED

Our host, darling! My brother-in-law! Laura's
husband!

MAX

No! Don't tell me that's Augustus Merrick!

WINIFRED

It certainly is! Society's darling, leader of fashion,
the greatest catch of twenty-five years ago!

MAX

Good Lord!

[7]

WINIFRED

He does look rather sour, doesn't he? Let's leave him alone. When'd you get here?

MAX

[*Still looking at* AUGUSTUS.]
About ten minutes ago.

WINIFRED

[*Taking off her wraps.*]
Where's Laura?

MAX

That's just the point. I haven't seen a soul except him. I wasn't even sure this was the place. Are you sure you said Thursday?

WINIFRED

Absolutely. I wired Laura: "Like to renew old acquaintance. May I come to you Thursday? Max Lawrence."
[*Ringing.*]
Well, this is a royal welcome for a sister one hasn't seen for fifteen long years!

MAX

It's worse than that. It's a decidedly unpleasant predicament!

WINIFRED

Unpleasant? Beautiful house, beautiful weather, absent hostess, dead host—what more could you want?

MAX

But we can't be found like this. We go to all the trouble of coming down separately and now here we are together.

WINIFRED

Exactly. I told you you should have come with me. I had a gorgeous drive down. You'd have loved it.

MAX

I know but—

WINIFRED

No you don't. Stuffed up in the train.

MAX

I got off the train up the line at a little town called Starkville and hired a car.

WINIFRED

I was furious at you for not coming with me. It's stupid of you to be so cautious.

MAX

I don't think so. I tell you I don't want Laura to know about us.

[9]

WINIFRED

But, Max, if you haven't seen Laura for twenty-five years what possible reason can you have for giving a damn what she thinks about anything? I've been wondering all the way down.

MAX

It's inconsiderate. People don't like to have their homes used for rendezvous. It's imposing and insulting.

WINIFRED

But why wouldn't you just as soon insult and impose on Laura?

MAX

I don't like to do that to anyone. Let alone a woman I was once fond of.

WINIFRED

You know, I believe Laura used to be your mistress.

MAX

Oh, you do?

WINIFRED

It's the only explanation I can see. I may be wrong.

MAX

You certainly are. I couldn't have been more than twenty and Laura around twenty-three. Girls of twenty-three aren't the mistresses of boys of twenty.

[10]

WINIFRED

Oh, no?

MAX

Well, they weren't twenty-five years ago. Anyway Laura wasn't. She didn't think any more of me than of the other boys she had hanging around her. Oh, some perhaps. We may have been in love a little— as children are. Really, we were just comrades.

WINIFRED

Just comrades! Now isn't that sweet?

MAX

Damn it all, it *was* sweet—as I remember. It was one of those things that have a certain glamour around them always.

WINIFRED

So much glamour, in fact, that I talked about her for two whole days before you realized you'd ever known her.

MAX

I had nearly forgotten—But waiting here in her own home—and now seeing him—sort of brought it back to me. And then, you know, coming down on the train I saw a girl who reminded me of her.

WINIFRED

Oh, been looking at little girls on trains again, have you?

[11]

MAX

She was crying—

WINIFRED

Poor child!

MAX

Well, anyway, I don't want Laura to think I've come to renew an old acquaintance and then find out I've just come to meet you here.

WINIFRED

All right, have it your own way. If anyone comes you can tell them that there's a strange, unknown and very dusty woman upstairs in the bath.

MAX

I'll tell them nothing. And you'll meet me as though I were nobody you'd ever seen before.

WINIFRED

Anything you say, darling.
[SHE *starts out as there is a great noise in the hall. It is followed by a second.* MAX *and* WINIFRED *start and* AUGUSTUS *is seen to jump violently.*]

MAX

[*Dodging back.*]
What's that?

WINIFRED

Someone's home.

[12]

MAX

Look out. He's waking up.

AUGUSTUS

[*Roaring angrily.*]
Louis! Confound it! Louis!

LOUIS

[*In the hall.*]
Yes, sir. One moment, sir.

WINIFRED

Trapped!

MAX

Sit down. Be careful.

AUGUSTUS

[*Pushing doors open.*]
What the devil is that noise?

LOUIS

[*Off.*]
The expressman, sir, with Miss Leone's trunks.
They've come.

AUGUSTUS

[*Shambling to his feet.*]
Has Miss *Leone* come?

LOUIS

[*Off.*]
Not quite time yet, sir. Mrs. Merrick has gone to
meet her train.

[13]

WINIFRED

[*In a whisper.*]
Daughter.

MAX

Good Lord, have they a daughter?

WINIFRED

Had one for twenty years.

AUGUSTUS

[*Shambling into the room.*]
I've told you all your life never to make a noise like
that. This house is for thought and meditation. How
the devil can I meditate with a noise like that?

LOUIS

I'm very sorry, sir.

AUGUSTUS

Umpfh!

[AUGUSTUS *and* LOUIS *enter the room simultane-
ously.* LOUIS *is about the age of* AUGUSTUS *and
is dressed in elaborate livery which at present is
very disheveled. He is uncomfortable in it.
Entering the room at the same time they each
see* WINIFRED *and* MAX *at the same time and
stand staring at them stupidly.*]

WINIFRED

Gussy, you old bear, you haven't changed the least
little bit!

[14]

AUGUSTUS

[*Eyeing her.*]
Seen you before somewhere.

WINIFRED

Don't you *know* me, Gussy? Aren't you expecting
me?

[*She runs to him and throws her arms around his
neck kissing him heartily.*]

AUGUSTUS

Right on the nose, by God! Get away from me.

WINIFRED

But Gussy, I'm *Winifred!* Oh, you old dear, I believe you know perfectly well who I am. You just
want to be petted.

AUGUSTUS

[*Breaking away.*]
My own house— Strange woman—Strange man—

WINIFRED

Do you really mean you don't remember your little
Winny-Winky? Your own sister and you haven't seen
her for fifteen years.

AUGUSTUS

Haven't got a sister.

WINIFRED

I'm really not your sister, am I? Would Laura be
angry if I kissed you once more—?

AUGUSTUS

[*Backing up.*]
Ho! The bigamist!

WINIFRED

Darling, is that what you call me? But I'm really
not. I've been ever so legal about marriage.

AUGUSTUS

Eight husbands, by God!

WINIFRED

Oh, dear no. Only three. And I still have the last
one.

AUGUSTUS

Is that him?

MAX

No—no. My name is—

AUGUSTUS

How'd you get in?

MAX

Walked in. I rang and no one answered—

AUGUSTUS

What d'ye want?

MAX

Well, if I'm not expected I can easily go—

WINIFRED

Gussy, where are your manners? This man is a guest.

AUGUSTUS

We don't have guests. What's been going on here?

LOUIS

[Who was addressed.]
I don't know, sir. I was told to go upstairs and put on this uniform.

AUGUSTUS

[Eyeing him.]
What've you got yourself into, you idiot?

LOUIS

[Uncomfortable.]
It's a footman's livery, sir. Mrs. Merrick had me put it on.

AUGUSTUS

What the devil for?

LOUIS

She's expecting a distinguished visitor and—

AUGUSTUS

Eh? What? Who?

LOUIS

Mr. Max Lawrence, sir. She thinks he'll be on this train—

[17]

WINIFRED

He's here already, Gussy.

AUGUSTUS

Where?

MAX

Here. I'm Max Lawrence. I'm sorry if I've inconvenienced anyone. I got off the train at Starkville so I'm afraid Mrs. Merrick won't meet me at the station.

AUGUSTUS

How could she if you're here?

MAX

Yes. That's exactly what I mean.

AUGUSTUS

Umpfh!

LOUIS

Your room is ready, sir; and yours, Madam if you'd care to see them.

WINIFRED

Thank you, Louis.

AUGUSTUS

I want to speak to you a minute, my dear.

WINIFRED

Of course, Gussy.

[18]

MAX

Well, I'll just go up and wash if you don't mind.

AUGUSTUS

Go wash. Go wash.

WINIFRED

I'll see you later, Mr. Lawrence.
[MAX *and* LOUIS *go out.*]

AUGUSTUS

Who's that fellow?

WINIFRED

Max Lawrence, Gussy. Haven't you ever heard of him? He's a very well known artist. A painter. And he's an old friend of Laura's.

AUGUSTUS

How do you know?

WINIFRED

He told me so himself. I came in and found him waiting and you sleeping so we waited together. He seems very nice.

AUGUSTUS

Damned impertinent loafer, that's what he is! What are you doing here?

WINIFRED

You're being rather ungentlemanly, Gussy. Weren't you expecting either of us?

[19]

AUGUSTUS

D'ye think I'd let you come if I had?

WINIFRED

I wrote Laura and Mr. Lawrence said he wired her.

AUGUSTUS

Never heard anything about it.

WINIFRED

Well, here we are anyway.

AUGUSTUS

And you're here for no good reason. I know your kind. They don't like the country.

WINIFRED

I must say that after fifteen years—

AUGUSTUS

Fifteen years be blowed. I won't have my house turned into a den for loose women and long-haired donkeys—

WINIFRED

You talk as though I were a devil. It isn't exactly pleasing.

AUGUSTUS

I don't mean to offend you. But I know the life you come from. Leone is coming home from college.

Don't want her to get any nonsense in her head.
Understand?

WINIFRED

But I'm not going to hurt Leone.

AUGUSTUS

Going to make something out of her. All rot about
having to know the world. In the world but not of it.
Understand?

WINIFRED

Gussy, how can you talk this way to your little
Winny-Winky? Have you forgotten how frightfully
I was in love with you when you married Laura?

AUGUSTUS

You were nothing but a little brat when I married
Laura.

WINIFRED

But awfully precocious, darling.
    [*Throws arms around him and kisses him.*]

AUGUSTUS

    [*Struggling.*]
Damnation! Absolutely depraved! Got to get you
out before Leone—
    [*He breaks away as* LAURA *bustles in from the
    hall. She is about forty-eight but has obviously
    tried to preserve an earlier age. She is extrava-
    gant in talk and gesture.*]

LAURA

Oh, my dear, my dear, something positively wicked has happened— Oh, pardon me, pardon me, I thought you were alone.

WINIFRED

Laura! Don't tell me that you don't know me either.

LAURA

Angel, is it really you? How wonderful to see you again.

[*She embraces* WINIFRED *eagerly.*]

I'm positively an animal the way I forget names. But your face—! Well, my dear, I remember your face as though it were my own!

AUGUSTUS

Umpfh!

WINIFRED

[*Breaking away.*]

You don't know me at all! I must say that after not having seen your own sister for over fifteen years—

LAURA

Winky! It's my own little Winky!

[*She gathers her in a hurried embrace.*]

To think that after all these years I again press my own flesh and blood. Augustus, it's our own little Winky!

[*She lets her go.*]

Pardon me, dear, but I simply mustn't cry. I'll ruin myself. Augustus, it's Winky!

AUGUSTUS

Know damn well it's Winky.

LAURA

But however did you get here? The last train is just in.

WINIFRED

I motored down.

LAURA

Oh, of course. Your letter came, dear, and I was so thrilled I was going to see you again. But I was so upset about something— Oh, I must tell you all about it. My dream! My one last dream! Oh, poor Augustus! Poor dear Augustus!

AUGUSTUS

What the devil's the matter with you today, Laura?

LAURA

You'll known soon enough.

[*To* WINIFRED.]

Pet, pet, you must tell me all about China or Chile or wherever you've been so long— And those husbands! Just imagine, Augustus calls you the bigamist. Isn't that too delicious? And John— It is John now, isn't it?

WINIFRED

John.

LAURA

I knew it was John. Henry was the one before. How is John?

WINIFRED

John's well.

LAURA

So sad he couldn't come too. And all those fascinating experiences you've been through. While I—! I've been simply withering away. Haven't I, Augustus? Withering away.

AUGUSTUS

I don't know what you're talking about.

LAURA

There, you see, Winky? He doesn't even understand. He does nothing but read and sleep—

AUGUSTUS

What d'ye mean? You know I can't sleep.

LAURA

Oh, yes you can. I caught you sleeping under the vinegar tree the other day. Vinegar tree, Winky! Fancy my knowing about a vinegar tree!

AUGUSTUS

Where's Leone?

LAURA

Oh, I forgot all about her! Just like I forgot your letter, darling. It came and I was so thrilled I was going to see you again. But I was so upset—

AUGUSTUS

Poor dear Augustus!

LAURA

Now don't be dismal, dear. Please don't be dismal.

AUGUSTUS

What d'ye mean by inviting a houseful of people when Leone is here? Young girl in college'll never keep her head thrown in with them.

LAURA

I don't understand you in the least.

AUGUSTUS

Young girl and a woman with eight husbands and some damn fool artist—

LAURA

Oh, you're being perfectly mysterious. Unless Louis told you about Mr. Lawrence—

AUGUSTUS

You know I mean Lawrence.

[25]

LAURA

[*To* WINIFRED.]
Max Lawrence, my dear, an old very dear friend of mine in the days when I was different. He must be motoring down too.

WINIFRED

Really?

LAURA

You're going to adore him. He's a musician, darling. A very famous pianist. I knew him while he was still practicing.

WINIFRED

Oh, he's a pianist?

LAURA

Oh, a very famous one!
    [AUGUSTUS *has looked up at* WINIFRED *and seeing that she is trying not to laugh has broken into a chuckle.*]
I don't see what you're laughing at, Augustus. Anyone but you would have heard of him. And to think, Winky, I haven't heard of him once in all these years.

AUGUSTUS

Then how the devil d'ye know he's famous?

LAURA

Really, dear, I believe you're trying to offend me. And I think he composed too, Winky.

WINIFRED

Oh, he probably did.

LAURA

Yes, he must have. The most divine music! I think I can still hear it. I inspired him, he said.

AUGUSTUS

Pianist!

LAURA

Pianists can be inspired as well as anyone else.

AUGUSTUS

Umpfh!

LAURA

There are some things in the world you'll never be able to understand, Augustus. Beyond good and evil. That is Art. What a stunning lipstick, Winky. Is it indelible?

WINIFRED

As much as any indelible lipstick.

AUGUSTUS

Where's Leone?

LAURA

Weeping. It breaks my heart. All the way from the station she wept on my shoulder. Oh, Winky, if you only had a daughter to weep on your shoulder. It's the most fascinating—

[27]

AUGUSTUS

What's wrong with her?

LAURA

My dear, he didn't ask her!

AUGUSTUS

What?

LAURA

He didn't ask her, my dear. And she was positive he was going to before college closed.

AUGUSTUS

What the devil are you talking about?

LAURA

Leone, Augustus! She was very nearly engaged. Her letters have been full of it. Such a nice boy, too. And such a family! She sent me his tree. But now it's vacation and she's home and he hasn't asked her.

AUGUSTUS

[*Glaring at her.*]
Never heard anything about it.

LAURA

Oh, oh, I must have forgotten to tell you. But now that nothing came of it, it's just the same anyway. How things do take care of themselves.

[LEONE *enters.*]
Oh, here you are, pet. Feeling better?

[28]

LEONE

Yes, thank you. Hello, Father.

AUGUSTUS

Hello, my dear.

[*She kisses him.*]

LEONE

How's the liver? Are you laying off beef and wine?

LAURA

Of course he isn't. He'll kill himself one of these days. Oh, well, what will happen will happen. Oh, this is your Aunt Winifred, darling. Winky—Leone.

WINIFRED

Hello, child. Heavens, how you've grown!

LEONE

How nice to see you again. I don't remember you much, of course, but I've heard Father speak of you so often that—

LAURA

Yes, yes, we won't go into that, pet.

WINIFRED

No, perhaps we'd better not.

LEONE

Are you going to be here long?

[29]

WINIFRED

A week if you'll have me.

AUGUSTUS

A week!

LEONE

I'm so glad. There're a million questions I want to ask you.

AUGUSTUS

What the devil d'ye mean by trying to get yourself engaged?

LAURA

Please, Augustus, please! Winky is here.

WINIFRED

Oh, don't mind me. I love a row.

LAURA

Winky! What a perfectly gloomy way of putting it!

WINIFRED

Not at all. It makes it so homey.

AUGUSTUS

Will you oblige me by answering my question?

LEONE

Well, I didn't get engaged, Father. Geoffry thinks I'm altogether too ignorant to get married.

[30]

AUGUSTUS
Geoffry!

LAURA
Ignorant? After a year in college? But what has that to do with it, pet? You don't have to know anything to get married. Isn't she the quaintest thing?

LEONE
Mother, I wish you wouldn't laugh at me. I'm terribly self-conscious and it hurts me to be laughed at.

LAURA
I'm not laughing at you, pet; just at your character.

LEONE
[*To* WINIFRED.]
You know how it is at my age. When someone older condescends to me I always remember how young I am and that I'm still a virgin and that's annoying to any intelligent girl.

LAURA
Leone!

AUGUSTUS
[*Weakly.*]
God Almighty!

LEONE
Well, isn't it? When you were my age didn't you feel the same way about it?

[31]

LAURA

How can I possibly be expected to remember a thing like that!

LEONE

Geoffry says there's no excuse for a girl's being a virgin.

AUGUSTUS

Will you stop saying that word?

WINIFRED

But Heavens, Leone! Who is this Geoffry?

LAURA

Geoffry Cole, Winky. The boy who didn't ask her. Isn't it breath-taking, having a daughter in a college?

LEONE

Mother, I wish you wouldn't keep throwing College up to me. Goodness knows it's hard enough for me to realize how I've been sheltered and protected—

AUGUSTUS

Where'd you get all this nonsense?

LEONE

It isn't nonsense. Geoffry says that's exactly the trouble with me. I'm too young and cold. Geoffry says that any girl, in order to know what true and lasting love is, must have loved and suffered and come out with an understanding and something fine.

AUGUSTUS

Geoffry says that!

WINIFRED

I think Geoffry must be adorable!

LEONE

[*Impulsively.*]

Oh, he is adorable. Sometimes I feel like his mother.

LAURA

Oh, my God! How could you possibly know what it feels like to be a mother. What an imagination!

LEONE

[*Tearfully.*]

Mother, must you make light of my feelings?

AUGUSTUS

Stop making light of her feelings.

LAURA

Pardon me, dear. Pardon me.

LEONE

Geoffry says I have them.

WINIFRED

Of course you have.

LEONE

Well, there's your answer, Mother.

[33]

LAURA

I didn't ask anything, pet.

LEONE

You asked why I said I was too ignorant. Geoffry
says that where either of the participants is ignorant
marriage is doomed to failure. So naturally he didn't
ask me.

LAURA

But I thought he didn't love you any more.

LEONE

Mother, how can you say such a thing! He wor-
ships me!

LAURA

Oh, I don't understand it at all. Do you, Winky? I
naturally supposed if he didn't ask her it was because
he didn't love her any more.

LEONE

[Sobbing.]
He'll always love me. Always, always, always! He
said so himself.

LAURA

Oh, my God, she's crying again.

AUGUSTUS

What don't you know enough about?

LEONE

Men! I don't know enough about men. I haven't
loved and suffered and come out—

[*The rest is lost in sobs.*]

LAURA

But, darling, you don't mean that Geoffry has given
up his first love just because you're innocent?

LEONE

But Geoffry and I have never loved anyone else before and Geoffry says one merely learns from first love
so it must be unhappy.

LAURA

Oh, he's wrong. He's wrong. It's the most beautiful one.

WINIFRED

I didn't find it so.

LAURA

Oh, yes, it is, Winky! It's the one you must hold
on to no matter what else happens. Oh, I must tell
you all about—

[*She stops from delicacy.*]

LEONE

No, I think he's right. I've been thinking about it
all the way home. I *am* cold. I'm nervous and suppressed and all tied up. But I don't intend to stay in
this state any longer.

[35]

AUGUSTUS

What d'ye mean?

LEONE

I mean that I'm going to learn. I'm going to love and suffer and—

LAURA

But darling, you don't mean you're going to fall in love with someone else?

LEONE

I'm going to devote myself to just that. I've been educated along all the wrong lines.

LAURA

But— I don't understand. How far? That is— Oh, isn't it silly talking about it! How far do you intend to fall in love with someone else?

LEONE

All the way.

LAURA

Oh! Oh, Winky!

WINIFRED

Who's the man?

LEONE

I don't know. I shall pick a gentleman who has loved and suffered—

AUGUSTUS

If you bring a man around here—

[36]

LEONE

[*With dignity.*]
Father! I've lost the man I love through sheer
ignorance and youth and I don't intend to do it again.

WINIFRED

It's really a charming idea though, Gussy.

LEONE

It's an intelligent one, don't you think?

AUGUSTUS

Damned nasty one, that's what it is.

LAURA

[*Suddenly laughing gaily.*]
No, it's really a *funny* one! Cute! That's it. Cute!

LEONE

[*Sobbing.*]
It isn't cute. I think you're all horrid to laugh at me.
[*She runs out hall door.*]

AUGUSTUS

Damnation! Now you've made her cry again.

LAURA

It won't hurt her, Augustus. She's used to it. Don't
annoy her.

[37]

AUGUSTUS

Don't try to order me, Laura. I'll annoy her if I want to.

[*He follows* LEONE *out.*]

LAURA

Augustus simply doesn't understand the child at all. Of course he was never a mother. He thinks college is some sort of cold-storage plant where you come out just like you went in except colder. Well, here we are, Winky. Isn't it curious?

WINIFRED

What?

LAURA

Your being here.

WINIFRED

Is it? You're my sister.

LAURA

But when anyone, especially one's own sister comes to see her for the first time in over five years—

WINIFRED

It's been fifteen years.

LAURA

No? Really? I thought you said five.

WINIFRED

You see, I'm tired and a trifle lonely. I've come to rest and be quiet for awhile.

[38]

LAURA

I'm sure you have, darling. And we're going to have a perfectly wonderful time. Leone, if she ever gets dry—is such fun. And Max! Oh, Winky, I simply must tell you.

WINIFRED

That's what I'm waiting to hear.

LAURA

Lend me your handkerchief. Mine is quite sopped —with Leone. And I'm liable to burst into tears at any moment. My emotion, you remember, or have you forgotten my emotion?

WINIFRED

I remember it well.

LAURA

Winifred, when you were a little girl of ten or so— Oh, Augustus must never know. It would simply annihilate him. He must never know.

WINIFRED

Never through me.

LAURA

Oh, of course I know that, darling. Winifred—he was my sweetheart.

WINIFRED

Augustus?

LAURA

Max, my dear! Max!

WINIFRED

No! Really? You don't mean to say you had a sweetheart?

LAURA

[Offended.]
I'm sure I don't know what you mean by that!

WINIFRED

But you've always been such a respectable person, Laura!

LAURA

Oh, that's what I've led people to believe! But I don't think even you, Winky, would say that it was respectable for a woman to have a lover before she's married.

WINIFRED

Laura! You don't mean to say Mr. Lawrence was your lover?

LAURA

Oh, yes, yes, Winky! He was. My lover in fact and fancy.

WINIFRED

[Laughing.]
Nonsense!

LAURA

Oh, it was awful of me.

[40]

WINIFRED

I'm shocked, Laura. Definitely shocked.

LAURA

Oh, but I'd do it again, Winky. It was so beautiful! The memory of that first artistic afternoon has buoyed me through years of despair.

WINIFRED

Then why didn't you marry him?

LAURA

How could I have married him? He was a struggling young artist of twenty. And there was Augustus offering me a home. So I sacrificed myself for both of them; to my love, not to be a mill-stone; to Augustus, to make him happy.

WINIFRED

It was truly noble of you.

LAURA

No one will ever know quite how noble. Darling, you who have been married too much can know nothing about being married too little.

WINIFRED

I see. But what about Mr. Lawrence?

LAURA

Winky! On the very eve of my marriage something was decided that gave me the courage to face

[41]

the years before me. Oh, how that evening comes back to me!

WINIFRED

Well?

LAURA

He was waiting for me in his barren studio.

WINIFRED

Where was that?

LAURA

Oh, I don't know now. What difference does it make? I remember creeping up the stairs in the dark—

WINIFRED

And you heard him playing there alone—

LAURA

Probably. A pianist usually plays when his heart is breaking. Yes, yes, he must have been playing. Playing wonderfully! Putting all of his anguish into that melody.

WINIFRED

Which melody was it?

LAURA

Oh, Winky, how can I possibly remember that? It may not have been a melody. I only know that *he* was there—waiting for me. I entered his barren studio and he rose, trembling. His voice was hoarse

[42]

when he spoke. "Tonight you go from me," he said. "I go from you," I repeated. I couldn't trust myself to say more. And then I said, "But my heart remains in this barren studio with you."

WINIFRED

The studio was very barren, wasn't it?

LAURA

Oh, yes, Winky. All those boys had dreadful places. [*Quickly romantic again.*]
And as he stood there, trembling, he swore that some day he would be famous, recognized throughout the world. That his name would rank with—with—Mozart—and—and—Chopin—and—and—

WINIFRED

And Botticelli?

LAURA

[*Gratefully.*]
And Botticelli. And that when that day came he would come to claim me. And I vowed that if ever he came I would be ready.

WINIFRED

What?

LAURA

[*Drawing a telegram from her bosom.*]
Listen! "Like to renew old acquaintance stop may I come to you Thursday. Max Lawrence."

WINIFRED

Oh, my God!

LAURA

What?

WINIFRED

Oh, it's too much!

LAURA

Winifred, are you hysterical?

WINIFRED

I don't know whether I'm laughing or crying.

LAURA

That's just what hysterical *is,* pet. Here's your handkerchief. It may be crying.

WINIFRED

It's neither. It's anger. Laura, don't stand there and tell me you're serious.

LAURA

Winky!

WINIFRED

You're not really fool enough to think any man would do what you say?

LAURA

Winky, you don't know Max!

[44]

WINIFRED

What are you going to do?

LAURA

Oh, I'm all upset. What shall I do? Wouldn't it be wonderful to take my place again in the life I was meant for?

WINIFRED

Oh, it's all too fantastic! Will you show me my room?

LAURA

Winky!

WINIFRED

You've made this whole thing up. You know perfectly well that this Mr. Lawrence was never your lover and that you haven't thought of him once since you knew him until that telegram came.

LAURA

I've dreamed of him night and day!

WINIFRED

You can't even remember where he lived.

LAURA

A detail, Winky, a detail.

WINIFRED

You don't even know he's famous.

LAURA

Oh, he is! He is!
  [*Terror-stricken.*]
Isn't he? Haven't you ever heard of him?

WINIFRED

Of course I've heard of him but—

LAURA

Of course you have, darling. It just shows how dead
I've been all this time. But there! You asked to see
your room. Where is your luggage? I never thought
to ask.

WINIFRED

I left most of it in the car.

LAURA

I've given you a room that looks right over the
garden. I remembered that when you were a little
girl you loved flowers.

WINIFRED

  [*Wandering to windows.*]
Did I? Anyway, it's a lovely garden. I noticed it
coming up.

LAURA

It belongs to Augustus. He'll probably bore you
with it.

WINIFRED

How wonderfully peaceful it is here.

[46]

LAURA

[*As* LOUIS *enters.*]

The peace of the grave, pet; the peace of the grave.

[*She goes to* LOUIS *and straightens his livery.*]

Yes, it looks nice. Be free in it, Louis. Perfectly free.

LOUIS

Yes, Mrs. Merrick.

LAURA

Did you take Mrs. Mansfield's luggage out of the car?

LOUIS

It's in the side room—

LAURA

All right. Show Mrs. Mansfield— Mansfield! Isn't that right, Winky?

WINIFRED

Perfect.

LAURA

Yes. John Mansfield. Henry Upjohn. I get confused. Show Mrs. Mansfield where it is, Louis.

LOUIS

Yes, Mrs. Merrick.

[LEONE *enters.*]

LAURA

Better again, darling?

[47]

LEONE

Yes, thank you.

LAURA

I'll be up in a minute to see that everything's all right, Winky.

WINIFRED

Don't bother. I'm sure it is.

LEONE

Mother, who is that man upstairs?
[LOUIS *is off;* WINIFRED *waits in doorway.*]

LAURA

Man, darling? Is it your father?

LEONE

Don't be silly, Mother. I know my Father.

LAURA

Don't speak to me that way, Leone.

LEONE

It's the same man that sat across from me on the train.

LAURA

Pet, you don't really mean there's a strange man up-stairs?

LEONE

I'm sure it's the same man. He got off at Starkville.

[48]

LAURA

That's the little town just before this one, Winky.

WINIFRED

Yes, I know.

LEONE

And I think it's very funny that he should be up-stairs now, don't you? He was just coming out of the bathroom.

LAURA

He's a criminal. I know he's a criminal. He's after some soap to plug up the telephone. He saw you and followed—

WINIFRED

Laura, can't you think of anyone it might be?

LAURA

How on earth could I know who gets off at Stark-ville?

WINIFRED

But someone it might be. Aren't you expecting any-one?

LAURA

Oh, Leone's got me so excited! Starkville? Stark-ville?

WINIFRED

It's Mr. Lawrence, Laura.

LAURA

It's Max!

[49]

WINIFRED

Yes. He was here when I came. You were expecting him, weren't you?

LAURA

It's Max! After all these years and I'm a ruin. Why in the world didn't you tell me he was here?

WINIFRED

I wanted a minute with you myself.

LAURA

I'll have Louis send him right down. You stay here and entertain him, Winky.

WINIFRED

I'll be back in a minute. Leone is here.
   [*She goes.*]

LAURA

Oh, I must fly. I must fly.

LEONE

Is he a friend of yours, Mother?

LAURA

Is he a friend of mine!
   [*She laughs gaily.*]
Is he a friend of mine!
   [*She becomes suddenly tragic.*]
Oh, my poor child! My poor child!
   [*She goes out to hall.*]

[LEONE *looks after her a moment, puzzled. As she turns into the room, a young man, covered with dust, wearing a dirty top coat, sticks his head in from the porch.*]

GEOFFRY

Are you alone?

LEONE

Geoffry! Oh my God, Geoffry, what are you doing here?

GEOFFRY

[*Entering rapidly.*]
I just came down.

LEONE

[*Starting to sob.*]
But I thought I wasn't going to see you again.

GEOFFRY

I changed my mind.

LEONE

[*Sobbing louder.*]
But I thought I wasn't going to see you again ever!

GEOFFRY

Don't cry.

LEONE

I can't help it.

GEOFFRY

Of course you can.

[51]

LEONE

But I can't, I say. I've been crying ever since I left you.

GEOFFRY

You didn't leave me. I was in the coal car.

LEONE

What coal car?

GEOFFRY

The coal car of the train you were on.

LEONE

You mean you rode all the way here in a coal car? Oh, Geoffry!

GEOFFRY

It was the only way I could get here. Don't you remember I only had fifty cents.

LEONE

But why did you come?

GEOFFRY

[*With difficulty*].
Because I—because I love you.

LEONE

[*Sobbing louder.*]
Oh, Geoffry!
[*She runs to him and throws herself into his arms.*]

[52]

GEOFFRY

Be careful!
[*He suddenly hugs her.*]

LEONE

But I thought I wasn't ever going to see you again.

GEOFFRY

When I saw your train pulling out I decided I couldn't let you go.

LEONE

Oh, Geoffry!

GEOFFRY

So I ran ahead and jumped in the coal car.

LEONE

The coal car! Oh, Geoffry!
[*They cling to each other.* LEONE *is sobbing.* GEOFFRY *is moved also. Pause.*]

GEOFFRY

First love is always messy like this.

LEONE

It's awful.

GEOFFRY

Everyone says youth is a beautiful time.

LEONE

It's ugly.

[53]

GEOFFRY

Sordid.

LEONE

And so humiliating!
  [*Pause.*]

GEOFFRY

Finished?

LEONE

I guess so.

GEOFFRY

So'm I.

LEONE

You'd better wash up before the others come down.

GEOFFRY

Others?

LEONE

Father and Mother. And then my Aunt Winifred is here and a man by the name of Max Lawrence.

GEOFFRY

The artist?

LEONE

I don't know. Is he an artist?

GEOFFRY

If it's the same one. A painter. Very popular now. I don't want to meet him.

LEONE

I guess you'll have to.

[54]

GEOFFRY

I don't want to meet any of them.

LEONE

Well, I don't see how you can get out of it.

GEOFFRY

I can never talk when there's more than one person in the room. Makes me self-conscious.

LEONE

You'll have to eat dinner with them.

GEOFFRY

I'd rather starve.
[*Pause. He looks around the room.*]
I didn't know your father had so much money.

LEONE

Father's got loads of money.

GEOFFRY

Why does he live way out here then?

LEONE

I don't know. I guess he likes it.

GEOFFRY

That's funny.
[*Pause.* LEONE *waits.*]

[55]

LEONE

Well, I'm awfully glad you came, Geoffry. Even if I don't know why exactly.

GEOFFRY

I've been thinking things over.

LEONE

[*Eagerly.*]
Have you, Geoffry?

GEOFFRY

Yes.

LEONE

Oh.
[*Pause. LEONE waits.*]
Well, what sorts of things did you think over?

GEOFFRY

Marriage.

LEONE

Oh.
[*Pause. LEONE waits.*]
You've been thinking a lot about marriage lately, haven't you?

GEOFFRY

Well, it's a very important matter, don't you think?

LEONE

[*Hastily.*]
Oh, yes. I do, Geoffry.
[*Pause. GEOFFRY thinks. LEONE waits.*]

[56]

GEOFFRY

I still think it's stupid for a girl to get married until she's had plenty of experience, you know.

LEONE

Yes. I know.

GEOFFRY

The idea is sound.

LEONE

Yes, I suppose it is.

GEOFFRY

But you see I love you and can't keep away from you.

LEONE

[*Rising.*]
Oh, darling!

GEOFFRY

Be careful.

[LEONE *sits. Pause.*]
It's a damn shame I didn't meet you a few years from now. You'll probably grow into a lovely woman.

LEONE

Do you think so, Geoffry?

GEOFFRY

There's no doubt of it. There'd be no resisting you.

LEONE

I know I'm incomplete as it is.

[57]

GEOFFRY

It's too bad.

LEONE

Yes.

[*Pause.* GEOFFRY *thinks.*]

GEOFFRY

But you see I love you.

LEONE

Yes, I know.

GEOFFRY

It's too bad.

LEONE

Yes.

[*Pause.*]

GEOFFRY

I think women should have that mellowness. It charms me.

LEONE

Well, I admitted I wasn't perfect, Geoffry.

GEOFFRY

That doesn't change it.

LEONE

[*Sharply.*]
Well, I'm terribly sorry.

GEOFFRY

I can just see you a few years from now: beautiful, intelligent, honest—like you are now; but, in addition,

[58]

you'll have learned to be graceful and gentle and understanding instead of self-conscious and awkward and obvious. There are some women who—

[WINIFRED *enters from hall.* GEOFFRY *stares at her.*]

LEONE

Oh, Winifred. This is Geoffry.

WINIFRED

[*Going to him.*]
The man with those stunning ideas! What a treat!
[*She shakes hands cordially.*]

GEOFFRY

[*To* LEONE.]
There! That's what I mean. Gracious. You'd have said, "Pardon me. I didn't catch the name." Something obvious.

WINIFRED

Who would have said that?

LEONE

[*Bitterly.*]
I would have.

GEOFFRY

Pardon my being dirty. I rode in the coal car.

WINIFRED

Well, my dear man, I should think you did! Just look at you.

GEOFFRY

[*Delighted.*]
See, Leone? Graceful. Mellow.

WINIFRED

Do you often ride in coal cars?

GEOFFRY

All the time, except the day I get my allowance.

WINIFRED

How romantic! You must have been on the same
train with Leone and Mr. Lawrence. What a lark!
By the way, dear, he spoke of seeing you.

LEONE

Really?

WINIFRED

He didn't know who you were but you made quite
an impression on him. He thinks you're adorable.

LEONE

Well! What do you make of that, Geoffry?

GEOFFRY

Adorable isn't anything.

LEONE

I'll show you if it isn't anything.

WINIFRED

[*To* GEOFFRY.]
He's probably just a silly elderly man who falls for young girls. Let's not bother with him.

GEOFFRY

[*To* LEONE.]
I think I'll stay to dinner after all.

LEONE

Oh, thanks so much, Winifred. I was trying to get him to stay.

WINIFRED

Of course he's going to stay. I'd be bored to death if he didn't. And I want to hear all those ideas of yours.
    [*She sees* LAURA *in hall.*]
Oh!
    [GEOFFRY *turns as* LAURA *enters from hall.*]

LAURA

Max! Max!
    [*She advances with outstretched hands.*]
After all these years!

LEONE

This is Geoffry, Mother.

LAURA

Geoffry?

LEONE

Geoffry Cole. The boy I told you about.

LAURA

Oh, my dear, he looks just like Max. The way Max used to look. I forgot for a moment. How do you do, Mr. Cole? But where is Max?

WINIFRED

I just saw him upstairs talking to Gussy. He'll be right down.

LAURA

So this is Geoffry. My, my, how dirty he is!

WINIFRED

He rode in the coal car.

LAURA

The Cole car? Your own private car, Mr. Cole?

LEONE

Don't try to be funny, Mother.

LAURA

Just a little pun. Just a little pun! My little girl—! And so he's asked you after all.

LEONE

Mother! Please! He followed me down here for no reason at all.

[62]

LAURA

I'm sure there's a reason.

[Louis *enters from hall.*]

Summer! Youth! Love! Oh, one's first love—

LOUIS

Mr. Max Lawrence.

LAURA

Oh, my God!

[Max *enters.* Laura *goes to him.*]

Max! Max! After all these years! I would have known you anywhere. Isn't it perfectly wonderful? Have I changed? And you've been upstairs all the time. No one ever told me. Oh, this is my sister, you know, whom I haven't seen for years. And here's Mr. Cole. He's something to do with my daughter. He's rather dirty now. And this is my daughter herself! Would you ever guess it. Leone, an old friend of mine, Max Lawrence.

LEONE

How do you do?

[Augustus *enters from hall.*]

MAX

[*Startled.*]

Oh! Why—! How do you do?

LEONE

I sat right across from you on the train coming down.

[63]

MAX

Yes, of course. I remember.

LAURA

Yes, wasn't it odd? And my husband, you know. You were talking to him upstairs.

MAX

Well, he was talking to me.

AUGUSTUS

Umpfh!

LAURA

Well, I guess we've all met.

AUGUSTUS

[*Pointing at* GEOFFRY.]
Who's that?

LAURA

Oh, oh! My mistake. This is Mr. Cole, Augustus.

AUGUSTUS

Who the devil is Mr. Cole?

WINIFRED

Leone's friend, Gussy.

AUGUSTUS

It's that Geoffry, by God! I'll settle his hash!

WINIFRED

Shame on you, Gussy. Where are your manners?

[64]

AUGUSTUS

Umpfh!

LEONE

[*To* Max.]
You must have thought I was terrible on the train.
I guess I was the reason you got off at Starkville.

MAX

Not at all.

LEONE

I was crying all over the place. It had been bottled
up inside of me all the way home.

LAURA

Yes, we all know that, darling. And there wasn't a
soul to meet you, Max. I thought you'd be on the
train.

MAX

I wanted the ride through the country. But I came
right in. Mr. Merrick was sleeping so I didn't—

AUGUSTUS

What d'ye mean I was sleeping?

MAX

[*Frightened.*]
Weren't you?

WINIFRED

Yes, he was, Mr. Lawrence. He just likes to pretend
he wasn't.

[65]

MAX

Oh, I see.

LAURA

Oh, he was. I'm sure he was.

AUGUSTUS

You know nothing about it, Laura.

LAURA

I'm sure if they both saw you sleeping that's all there is to it. You must have been sleeping.

AUGUSTUS

They seem damn glad that I *was* sleeping.

WINIFRED

Why, Gussy, what do you mean?

LAURA

Oh, he doesn't mean anything. Don't mind him. He's always funny like that.

[*She takes* MAX's *arm.*]

Max, dear, I'm positively not going to give you a moment's rest until you've told me every single thing that has happened in the last twenty-five years. Have I changed, do you think?

MAX

Well, not materially.

[66]

WINIFRED

Still it has been twenty-five years, hasn't it?

LAURA

Of course I must have changed. Just a rhetorical question. And now you're famous! How well I remember that spirited young boy who first taught me to love art!

LEONE

Mr. Lawrence, are you going to be here long?

LAURA

[*To* LEONE.]
You'd better run up and unpack, don't you think, darling? Your dresses will get all mussed.

AUGUSTUS

Hear you're a famous pianist.

MAX

Oh, no. You see I'm a—

LAURA

Now don't be modest! Famous! Augustus, he's known the world over.

LEONE

Then you *are* the famous Mr. Lawrence?

LAURA

[*Gaily.*]
Of course he is, Leone. Are you just catching on to that?

[67]

LEONE

But you're not a pianist, are you? I thought Geoffry said that Max Lawrence was a painter.

[*There is a moment's pause.* Augustus *chuckles.*]

MAX

That's very nice of Geoffry. As a matter of fact, that is my job.

[Laura *sees her mistake.*]

AUGUSTUS

[*Chuckling at* Laura.]
Pianist! Pianist!

LAURA

[*Laughing gaily.*]
Why do you keep on saying, "Pianist, pianist?" Wherever did you get that idea, Augustus?

AUGUSTUS

Now look here, Laura—

LAURA

[*Brushing him aside.*]
Isn't he a scream?

[*To* Max.]

He's the most ignorant thing. Don't you simply adore Rembrandt? His best ones, you know. Of course he had a younger period.

AUGUSTUS

But you—

LAURA

I love all the old masters. Now take Holstein, for example. I simply worship him. By the way, someone the other day said that I reminded him of a Holstein. Is there anything in it?

[*She looks around, but hearing* AUGUSTUS *chuckle thinks something may be wrong, so she goes on, as the curtain falls.*]

I've posed for so many artists. There's something about me they try to catch. Oh, not in the nude, you know.

[*She laughs gaily.*]

I could never do that. Of course, I approve of it heartily. Art, you know—

[LEONE, *with a glance at* GEOFFRY, *who is staring at* WINIFRED, *takes* MAX's *arm, as—*]

[CURTAIN]

THE VINEGAR TREE

ACT TWO

ACT II

Same as Act I. After dinner.

LAURA *is being sketched by* MAX. *She sits rigid, very affected, an expression of girlish coyness in her face and position.* LEONE *is hanging over* MAX's *shoulder, watching him draw.* WINIFRED *stands looking out onto the porch which is bathed in moonlight.* AUGUSTUS *sits sprawled out in the center of the room, picking his teeth.* GEOFFRY, *very shy, sits in a corner, never taking his eyes from* WINIFRED. *They are all dressed, excepting* GEOFFRY. *As the curtain rises,* LOUIS *is finishing bringing in table with whiskey and soda, etc. They help themselves during the first scene.* LAURA *is talking in a nasal, unnatural voice, trying not to disturb her expression.*

LAURA

But you mustn't say anything but yes or no. That's very important. Do you understand it now?

MAX

[*Looking up.*]
Not very clearly. I'm rather poor at games.

[73]

LAURA

Oh, why didn't you say so? I loathe them. We won't play.

[*Silence.* MAX *sketches. No movement. Everyone is bored. Suddenly* AUGUSTUS *pulls his hand from his mouth and holds it out to* LAURA.]

AUGUSTUS

[*Booming.*]
Bone!
[*They all jump.*]

LEONE

Father! Now you've made him spoil her eye.

MAX

[*Erasing.*]
Never mind. I'll fix it.

AUGUSTUS

[*To* LAURA.]
Stuck right in my left molar. See?

LAURA

Now don't make me lose this expression, Augustus. Just be quiet for a moment.

AUGUSTUS

[*Feeling his tooth.*]
I've told you a million times that woman doesn't

[74]

know how to do crab-meat. Now I've got a sore tooth again.

[*Another silence.*]

WINIFRED

[*Turning in from window.*]
Well, are we going to play or aren't we?

LAURA

No, Winky. Max is perfectly right. One can't be creating art and playing games at the same time.

WINIFRED

I think Mr. Lawrence can understand it. It's quite simple.

MAX

Thank you.

WINIFRED

One of us goes out of the room and while he's gone the rest of us choose some object.

LAURA

Subject, Winky.

WINIFRED

Well, choose something. Then we call him in—

LAURA

The one we've sent out, you see, Max.

MAX

Yes. I get that.

WINIFRED

And he has to guess what we've chosen.

LAURA

In twenty questions.

AUGUSTUS

But he can only ask questions that can be answered by yes or no.

LAURA

Yes, that's very important. The rest of us mustn't answer anything but yes or no. Otherwise he'll guess it by guessing rather than logic.

WINIFRED

Do you understand it now?

MAX

I guess so. Go ahead and I'll catch on.

AUGUSTUS

[*Pointing suddenly at* GEOFFRY.]
Go out.

GEOFFRY

[*Taken unaware.*]
What?

AUGUSTUS

Go out. Leave the room.

GEOFFRY

What have I done?

[76]

WINIFRED

You said you knew the game, didn't you, Mr. Cole?

GEOFFRY

[*Blankly.*]
Game?

LEONE

[*Crossly.*]
Yes game! We're playing twenty questions. Perhaps you hadn't noticed.

GEOFFRY

Oh, I beg your pardon.
[*He goes out quickly.*]

AUGUSTUS

Young idiot!

LAURA

I don't know why you say that, Augustus. I think he's a very sweet boy. You've been treating him wretchedly, Leone.

LEONE

[*Ignoring her, leaning over* MAX.]
You're very expert, aren't you?

MAX

Oh, no. I'm really not much good at drawing.

LAURA

[*Sharply.*]
I spoke to you, Leone.

[77]

LEONE

I know I've treated him wretchedly.   He deserves it.

WINIFRED

I don't think he does.

LEONE

No, you wouldn't.

LAURA

Why do you do it?

LEONE

He had no right to come down here.

LAURA

[*Agitated.*]
Give him time, darling.   You must give him time.

AUGUSTUS

Why must she?   He's a young idiot.

LAURA

He isn't at all.   And one should never give up one s
first love.   Especially when they're so sweet.
[MAX *moves uncomfortably.*]

AUGUSTUS

Hasn't said a word since he's been here.

LEONE

He's self-conscious in some people's presence.
[*She looks at* WINIFRED.]
[78]

AUGUSTUS

He's what?

MAX

[*Looking up.*]
Self-conscious. Have you noticed, he doesn't say a word.

AUGUSTUS

I just said that.

MAX

Oh, did you?

AUGUSTUS

Yes I did.

LAURA

You don't need to be so touchy, Augustus.

AUGUSTUS

If there's anything makes me furious it's to have someone repeat after me just what I've said.

MAX

I beg your pardon. I was busy with this sketch.

LEONE

[*Leaning over* MAX *lovingly.*]
Isn't her nose a little fuller right here?

MAX

[*Surveying the sketch.*]
Is it?

LEONE

Right here. Shouldn't it come out like this?

MAX

I believe you're right. You've an eye for contour, haven't you?

LEONE

[*Softly.*]
Have I?
[*They smile at each other to* LAURA's *disgust.*]

LAURA

You know nothing about it, Leone. I'm sure Mr. Lawrence has made my nose as full as it should be.

WINIFRED

[*Looking over* MAX's *shoulder.*]
But where's that wistful expression, Mr. Lawrence?

MAX

What?

WINIFRED

You've made her too sophisticated. You haven't caught that shy and quiet wistfulness that was in her face.

AUGUSTUS

Umpfh!

MAX

I wish you wouldn't look over my shoulder. It distracts me.

WINIFRED

[*With a look at* LEONE.]
Really! I'd never have guessed it.

[80]

GEOFFRY

[*Putting his head in.*]
Are you ready?

LAURA

[*Laughing.*]
Oh, oh, we haven't chosen a subject yet. Just a
minute more, Mr. Cole.

[GEOFFRY *disappears.*]
Now what shall we choose?

WINIFRED

Let's choose this sketch.

LAURA

Oh, that's too easy. He'd guess that in no time.

AUGUSTUS

He'd never guess it.

LAURA

He'd guess it right off, Augustus. It's so obvious.

AUGUSTUS

He's an idiot, I tell you. He'd never guess it.

WINIFRED

Then let's take the gold medal Mr. Lawrence got
for his last painting.

LAURA

Oh, yes the prize. The one he was telling us about
at dinner. But I think the sketch would be better.

[81]

AUGUSTUS

We'll take the gold medal. Call him in.

WINIFRED

All right, Mr. Cole.

LAURA

Now one other thing. All keep perfectly straight faces and all keep perfectly silent except when it's your turn to answer and then only say yes or no. Don't speak out of turn—

AUGUSTUS

Shh—!

[GEOFFRY *enters.*]

LAURA

All right, Mr. Cole. We've chosen. Do you know the right questions to ask us?

GEOFFRY

I think so.

LAURA

All right. Start with Mrs. Mansfield.

[*Pause.* GEOFFRY *turns to* WINIFRED.]

GEOFFRY

[*Shyly.*]

Well— Is it concrete?

LAURA

Oh, I'd just take that for granted, Mr. Cole. I wouldn't—

AUGUSTUS

Shh—!

LAURA

But he's going to waste a question.

LEONE

Mother! Geoffry knows how to play.

LAURA

Oh, very well. Go on, Mr. Cole. But I'd never do it that way.

[*Pause.* GEOFFRY *is confused.*]

GEOFFRY

[*To* WINIFRED.]
Well— Is it concrete?

WINIFRED

Yes, concrete, Mr. Cole.

LAURA

Now nothing but yes or no, Winky.

AUGUSTUS

What the devil does it matter if she says his name?

LAURA

Why it matters a lot. Nothing but yes or no. That's the rule. Go on, Mr. Cole.

GEOFFRY

[*To* MAX.]
Is it—vegetable?

MAX

No.

LAURA

That's the way, Max. Just a simple direct "No."
Oh, oh, wouldn't you call it vegetable, though?

AUGUSTUS

Of course it's not vegetable.

LAURA

It certainly has vegetable in it.

LEONE

Oh, Mother!

AUGUSTUS

You said you weren't supposed to talk.

LAURA

But it isn't fair. You're putting him on the wrong
track.

WINIFRED

Oh, you're thinking of the wrong thing, Laura.
[*She whispers to her.*]

LAURA

Oh, no, no, Winky! We decided on the other.

WINIFRED

No. I suggested that first and you said it was too
easy. So we decided on the other.

[84]

LEONE

Mother, we decided on the second one Winifred suggested.

AUGUSTUS

Of course we did.

LAURA

You mean the —? Oh! I nearly gave it away. You mean we didn't choose the sketch?

LEONE

Of course we didn't.

LAURA

Oh, very well. I thought we had and that certainly has vegetable in it. Paper is vegetable. I was reading only the other day—

AUGUSTUS

Are we playing games or talking about what you read?

LAURA

All right. Go on, Mr. Cole. It's not vegetable. Not at all vegetable. Now ask me. I haven't answered yet.

AUGUSTUS

It's my turn.

LAURA

Ask him first, then, Mr. Cole.

GEOFFRY

Yes, ma'am.

[85]

LAURA

Oh, my dear boy, you don't have to call me ma'am.

WINIFRED

Oh, my God! Ask Mr. Merrick.

GEOFFRY

[*To* AUGUSTUS.]
Is it animal?

AUGUSTUS

Of course not. Animal!
[*He chuckles.*]
[*Pause.*]
[GEOFFRY *thinks.*]

GEOFFRY

Then it must be metal.

LAURA

That's right.

AUGUSTUS

What the devil d'you say that for?

LAURA

Well, he knows it's metal. If it isn't animal or vegetable it must be metal.

LEONE

It could be mineral.

LAURA

He knows we wouldn't choose a mineral.

[86]

AUGUSTUS

If you can't keep still I won't play.

LAURA

Oh, very well. Now it's my turn. Ask me, Mr. Cole.

GEOFFRY

Well, let me see. Is it a precious metal?

LAURA

Oh, yes, it must be. Isn't it, Max?

MAX

Yes.

AUGUSTUS

Good Lord, now you gave it away.

LAURA

What did I give away?

AUGUSTUS

You gave away it's something this fellow knows more about than the rest of us.

LAURA

Oh, you gave it away yourself just now. I might have asked that question of anyone. Just a general question. Now he knows it's something that belongs to Max.

AUGUSTUS

[*Furiously.*]

Oh, my God! Now he knows it *belongs* to him.

[87]

LAURA

Oh, don't be childish, Augustus.

AUGUSTUS

Childish be damned! You've given it all away.

LAURA

After all it's just a game.

AUGUSTUS

But I wanted to play it.

LAURA

All right. Go ahead. You don't know what it is, do you, Mr. Cole?

GEOFFRY

The only precious metal I know of that might belong to Mr. Lawrence is the prize he was speaking of at dinner.

AUGUSTUS

There!

LAURA

But it's wonderful! He guessed it in three questions. However did you do it? Now aren't you ashamed you called him an idiot, Augustus?

[*Embarrassed pause.* GEOFFRY *turns away.*]

LEONE

Mother!

[88]

AUGUSTUS

Really, Laura, you make the most unbelievable breaks.

LAURA

[*Quickly.*]

You know, this game is terribly popular all over New York. The best people are playing it. It's really too marvelous. To think of their doing something so worth-while, I mean—

AUGUSTUS

You're a dunce.

LAURA

[*Turning on him.*]

Don't you insinuate I'm a dunce. You did say he was an idiot. You know you did.

[GEOFFRY *starts to leave.*]

Oh, don't go, Mr. Cole.

[*To* AUGUSTUS.]

Now you've hurt his feelings.

AUGUSTUS

I didn't do it. You called him an idiot twice.

LAURA

I just repeated what you said. And I was covering it up beautifully. He'd never have noticed if you'd kept still. Would you, Mr. Cole?

[89]

GEOFFRY

Yes I would.

[*He goes out to porch.* LEONE *has been staring at him, sorrowfully.*]

LEONE

I think you're all terrible. Geoffry is very sensitive.

[*She starts to follow him out.*]

WINIFRED

You may have started some complex in him. I think I'd better go out and see.

LEONE

You don't have to.

WINIFRED

No trouble.

[*She goes out. Pause.* LEONE *returns to* MAX.]

AUGUSTUS

It was a bad break though, Laura. You're not as skilfull as you used to be.

LAURA

[*Ignoring him.*]
How is it coming, Max?

MAX

I'm nearly finished.

AUGUSTUS

One loses one's social graces as one gets older.

[90]

LAURA

[*Same.*]
Am I doing everything all right?

MAX

Yes. Fine.

AUGUSTUS

You might look natural for a minute.

LAURA

[*Turning on him.*]
I'm looking perfectly natural. That's just what I'm concentrating on.

AUGUSTUS

You're looking exceedingly silly, if I may say so.

LAURA

[*Jumping up.*]
Don't you dare speak to me that way, Augustus Merrick!

AUGUSTUS

You've looked and acted exceedingly silly all evening.

LAURA

Oh, you boor! You unspeakable boor! I won't stand it another minute.
[*She runs out to hall.*]

LEONE

Father, you have no right to speak to her that way.

[91]

AUGUSTUS

[*Rising.*]
I'll speak to her any way I choose.

LEONE

I think you're awful tonight.
[LEONE *turns away. Pause.* AUGUSTUS *glares at
her a moment, then looks at* MAX—*To* MAX.]
May I see it?

MAX

[*Who is getting his material together.*]
What? Oh! Yes, of course.
[*He gives the sketch to* AUGUSTUS. AUGUSTUS
studies it. Pause.]

MAX

[*Lamely.*]
It isn't much good.

AUGUSTUS

[*Bluntly.*]
You knew her when she was a girl.

MAX

Yes.

AUGUSTUS

Pretty little thing, wasn't she?

MAX

Charming.

AUGUSTUS

Natural. Unaffected.

[92]

MAX

Exactly.

AUGUSTUS

Umpfh! Something like Leone, don't you think?

MAX

Yes, now that you speak of it.

LEONE

What do you mean by that, Father?

AUGUSTUS

[*Giving her the sketch.*]
Now look at her.

LEONE

[*Turning away.*]
I know. I saw it.—Well, everyone gets older, don't they?

AUGUSTUS

Not like that.
[*To* MAX.]
Care for a high-ball?

MAX

No. Thank you.

AUGUSTUS

Anything?

MAX

I believe not.

AUGUSTUS

Ring for it if you do.
[AUGUSTUS *goes out to hall.*]

[93]

LEONE

Aren't we beastly?

MAX

Who?

LEONE

Who? All of us. Ill-mannered, ill-tempered, ill-everything. There's not a healthy one among us, especially Father.

MAX

He's rather bitter, isn't he?

LEONE

He's poisonous. And now that he's sick of life he makes everyone around him as disgruntled and disillusioned as he is. When I come back from college this way I see us all rather objectively and it disgusts me. I hate unhappy people. What are you smiling at?

MAX

Are you disgruntled and disillusioned?

LEONE

I'm becoming that way.

MAX

[*Laughing.*]
What a pity!

LEONE

Oh, you can laugh! But I'm precocious, and neurotic and all the rest of the things that go with—pampered people.

MAX

I think you're rather a dear.

LEONE

Well, I'm not. I'm just as obnoxious as the rest of them. I'm boring you. Is there anything in particular you'd like to do?

MAX

What, for instance?

LEONE

[*Wandering to windows.*]

We could go out in the garden. It's lovely there now. And there's a pool and a fountain and some what-nots.

MAX

All right.

LEONE

Oh, but Winifred and Geoffry are there. Unless you'd like to join them.

MAX

As a matter of fact, I'd rather not.

LEONE

I could show you my old playhouse, out in the grove. It's rather fun. We've got it all fixed up.

MAX

Must I be entertained?

LEONE

Well, after all the rows you've had to sit through I feel I should do something for you.

MAX

I'd be very happy just sitting here and talking to you.

LEONE

Would you really? All right.
[*They are standing by the window. She looks up at him. Their eyes meet. She moves over to the sofa with a nervous laugh.*]

MAX

[*Sitting by her.*]
You know, I didn't get off the train because you bothered me.

LEONE

Didn't you?

MAX

No. It was because I felt sorry for you and couldn't think of anything to do about it.

LEONE

How exciting!

MAX

And I've thought about you a lot since.

LEONE

You've thought I was fresh, I dare say.

[96]

MAX

Yes. Exactly. Very fresh and invigorating.

LEONE

That's because I'm young.

MAX

Is it? You have an answer for everything.

LEONE

You're probably used to blasé, sophisticated people.

MAX

I don't think about people much, as a rule.

LEONE

[*Looking up nervously.*]
But you did of me? Is that it?

MAX

Exactly.

LEONE

That was very sweet of you. I say, are you making love to me?

MAX

Perhaps a little. Not very strenuously—

LEONE

Because if you are it might be better to take our chances in the garden, after all.

[97]

MAX

Oh! Do you *want* me to make love to you?

LEONE

That's been perfectly obvious all evening, hasn't it?

MAX

I wasn't sure.

LEONE

Everyone else was.

MAX

Well, I'm glad I caught on in time.

LEONE

You know, you're lots different from what I first thought.

MAX

How?

LEONE

Well, when I saw you on the train of course I knew you had loved and suffered but I didn't think you'd be as sincere as you are.

MAX

I'm very sincere.

LEONE

I thought you were probably awfully blasé and sophisticated. You look that way.

MAX

Oh, Lord, do I? That's a drawback, isn't it?

[98]

LEONE

Not at all. For you're really quite simple. Do you mind?

MAX

Being simple?

LEONE

Yes.

MAX

Of course not. I *am* simple.

[GEOFFRY *enters from porch.*]

LEONE

What do you want?

GEOFFRY

Winifred wants her shawl.

LEONE

Winifred! Oh! Congratulations!

GEOFFRY

Why shouldn't I call her Winifred?

LEONE

No reason in the world.

GEOFFRY

She said it was on her bed.

LEONE

Why don't you get it for her?

[99]

GEOFFRY

I thought you might. You know the house better than I do.

LEONE

Hasn't Winifred told you where her bedroom was yet?

GEOFFRY

That's worthy of you.
[*He starts toward hall.*]

LEONE

It'll probably be chilly in the garden before morning.

GEOFFRY

It's chilly there now.
[*He goes out to hall.* LEONE *turns to* MAX *suddenly.*]

LEONE

[*Impulsively.*]
Mr. Lawrence, may I ask you something rather personal?

MAX

Please do.

LEONE

Are you a married man?

MAX

Why, no— Not exactly. That is— No. No. Not at all.

[100]

LEONE

Good. If you were married it would involve a third person and I don't want to do that.

MAX

Good Lord, this sounds rather serious.

LEONE

It is. I'm terribly nervous.

MAX

I'm sorry. Is there anything I can do?

LEONE

Yes. That's just it. But I don't know how to ask you.

MAX

Ask me perfectly frankly.

LEONE

You're a broad-minded person, aren't you?

MAX

I think so.

LEONE

I mean you don't always observe the strictest moral code yourself, do you?

MAX

Oh, Good Lord! What do you mean?
[*He glances uneasily toward garden.*]

[101]

LEONE

You're intelligent, artistic and kind. You aren't one of these people whose minds are all warped by puritanic principles, are you?

MAX

I'm not exactly a puritan, if that's what you mean.

LEONE

I'm sure you're not—being a painter. You see, puritans are such nasty people. They don't put the proper values on things. They have only one value. Sex. All they think of is sex.

MAX

Now out with it. What's worrying you?

LEONE

Very well. Mr. Lawrence, I am a virgin.

MAX

Oh, Lord!

LEONE

What's the matter?

MAX

Why, my dear Miss Merrick, I never doubted it for a moment. I assure you I had no intentions—

LEONE

Oh, you don't understand.

[102]

MAX

No, I guess not. I hope that nothing I've said—
I may have become sentimental for a moment—

LEONE

Don't be silly. I know you're not trying to take
advantage of me. I'm just telling you.

MAX

But, my dear girl, you don't have to explain yourself to me.

LEONE

But I *want* to. I believe you're shocked.

MAX

Well, I must confess to a little embarrassment.

LEONE

That just shows how much I know about men. It
never entered my mind that an *artist* would be
shocked by the word "virgin."

MAX

I suppose it's a matter of getting used to it.

LEONE

Haven't you ever heard it before?

MAX

I've never had a girl give me that information about
herself.

LEONE

That's because a girl's ashamed of being one. Geoffry says it's an unintelligent state to be in.

MAX

Oh, look here, you don't mean, this Geoffry *objected* to your being a—a—

LEONE

[*Eagerly explaining.*]
Of course he did. I'm very cold you see.

MAX

Of course I didn't know.

LEONE

You might have guessed. I'm cold because I'm suppressed.

MAX

Yes. That's too bad.

LEONE

I think about sex all the time. But I shouldn't. I want to put it in its proper place so that I'll have time to think of other more important things.

MAX

And you—? I'm a little bewildered.

LEONE

Well, my mind is fairly sophisticated for a girl of my age, don't you think?

[104]

MAX

Oh, yes. I certainly agree with you there.

LEONE

But my body is so naïve it disgusts my mind. See what I mean?

[*She looks at him earnestly. Pause.*]

MAX

Well, I'm afraid I do.

LEONE

[*Quickly.*]
I'm boring you.

MAX

On the contrary.

LEONE

Then I'm amusing you. That's worse.

MAX

Don't you want to amuse me?

LEONE

[*Tearfully.*]
Not when I'm being serious. That's just it. I *do* want to be amusing. I want to be witty, light, entertaining like Winifred. But how can I be with this weight on my shoulders? All I do is sit around and cry; act like a sad, earnest young thing. And I'm really not that sort at all.

[*She has become very excited. She is sobbing. Pause. She turns away.*]

[105]

MAX

Oh, look here. You mustn't upset yourself.

LEONE

[*Sobbing.*]
Don't mind me. It's only nerves.

MAX

I'm frightfully sorry.

LEONE

I know I'm disgusting.

MAX

You're not at all. I hate to see you cry.
[LEONE *looks up at him.*]

LEONE

[*Softly.*]
Do you really?

MAX

Of course I do.

LEONE

I wouldn't have told you all this only I thought
you'd understand—and that you liked me.

MAX

I do. A great deal.

LEONE

[*Softly.*]
A great deal?

[106]

MAX

It's been a long time since I've met anyone I liked
so much.

LEONE

I'm awfully glad.
[*Pause.* MAX *suddenly speaks in a low voice.*]

MAX

You don't really mean all this?

LEONE

I think so.

MAX

It would be simply mad of you.

LEONE

That's my lookout.

MAX

And this—Geoffry?

LEONE

Geoffry! That's finished!
[*Pause.*]

MAX

And your father and mother—

LEONE

They'd never find out.
[*Pause.*]

MAX

I'd be an awful cad, you know.

[107]

LEONE

I don't think you would.
  [*Pause.*]

MAX

You're damnably pretty.
  [*It looks as though he were going to take her into his arms.* LEONE *thinks so too.*]

LEONE

Let's go out in the garden after all.

MAX

  [*Checking himself.*]
All right.

LEONE

We can go out in my old playhouse and talk. We won't be disturbed there.

MAX

  [*Looking at her.*]
You're quite mad.

LEONE

I'll run up and get a wrap. Will you wait for me?

MAX

Yes.
  [*They look at each other a moment in silence. Then* LEONE, *with a nervous laugh goes toward hall as* WINIFRED *enters from porch.*]

WINIFRED

It gets surprisingly chilly out there among the hya-cinths.

MAX

[*Startled.*]

Oh! Oh, come in, Mrs. Mansfield. Mr. Cole has gone after your shawl.

LEONE

I'm just going up. I'll see what's keeping him.

WINIFRED

Thanks, dear. But I've got to go up anyway.

LEONE

Oh, that'll be much better. He probably can't de-cide which is your shawl and which your nightie.

[*She goes.*]

WINIFRED

Sweet little thing, isn't she?

MAX

Yes. Decidedly. And I must say you're being rather rotten to her.

WINIFRED

Uhmmmm?

MAX

Do you have to chase every young boy you see?

WINIFRED

Jealous?

MAX

If that's the reason you're doing it you can stop right now.

WINIFRED

It seems to me only fair Geoffry should have the pleasure of learning what Leone's going to learn.

MAX

What do you mean?

WINIFRED

Don't be surprised. She informed the whole family before dinner.

MAX

Well, I'll be damned. Look here, Winifred, I think it's outrageous. Leone's really a fine girl and this young Cole has put a lot of nasty ideas into her head.

WINIFRED

Well, what difference does it make to you?

MAX

It happens to make a great deal of difference to me.

WINIFRED

I see.

MAX

[*Uncomfortably.*]

I mean a thing like that should make a difference to everyone.

WINIFRED

Shocked?

MAX

Yes, I am. And I'm shocked at the way you seem to take it, too.

WINIFRED

We can't all be twenty.

MAX

We can all be decent.

WINIFRED

Wouldn't that be jolly.

MAX

You're not exactly a soft-hearted person, are you, Winifred?

WINIFRED

No. Of course not. Are you just finding that out?

MAX

Yes.

WINIFRED

What's the matter with you anyway? I come in with the most amiable intentions and you jump on me.

MAX

[*Wandering to windows.*]

Well, I've done a great deal of thinking just since I've been here.

WINIFRED

And I obviously didn't come out very well.

[111]

MAX

[*Looking onto the porch.*]

There's something about the country that makes one stop and think about himself.

WINIFRED

It's the air.

MAX

You know, I've the feeling I've been leading the wrong sort of life entirely.

[WINIFRED *laughs.*]

What's the matter?

WINIFRED

Nothing. That just struck me as funny.

MAX

Why?

WINIFRED

Don't you think you're being rather obvious, darling? And just slightly moral?

MAX

Well, you know, Winifred, I've been leading a hectic sort of existence, with husbands always in the background, and—

WINIFRED

And, damn it all, you're not that sort.

MAX

No. I'm not. Not that I object to it for others.

[112]

WINIFRED

Thanks. That's sweet of you.

MAX

But I'm a serious person. One needs to be blasé and sophisticated for that sort of thing. I'm really a simple person.

WINIFRED

Simple? That's right.

MAX

I hate intrigue. Now that I think of it I've always hated it. It takes too much time. I don't know how I ever got into these affairs anyway.

WINIFRED

We seduced you, Max.

MAX

Oh, look here, I didn't mean you.

WINIFRED

Of course you did. It's true.

MAX

It sounds rather egotistical, doesn't it?

WINIFRED

Does it? If I were a man I wouldn't feel hugely elated to think I could be made by any little girl that happened by.

[113]

MAX

What do you mean?

WINIFRED

Oh, don't be a fool, Max! Can't you talk two minutes to a little thing like Leone without letting her make a two-year-old out of you?

MAX

I rather resent that, Winifred.

WINIFRED

Oh, go to the devil.

MAX

I think to the garden if you don't mind.

WINIFRED

I'll send Leone out to you if I see her.

MAX

Thanks. That will be charming of you.
  [*He goes out to porch.* WINIFRED *stands looking after him a moment. Then shrugs, and starts to hall as* LAURA *enters, burdened down with pictures.*]

LAURA

Oh, my dear, I've found some perfectly priceless art things in an old box up in the billiard room. I want to get Max's opinion on them.

WINIFRED

He just stepped out on the porch.

LAURA

[*On the way to the sofa.*]

I don't suppose any of these are worth anything. Still I've had them so long. Help me with them, Winky. We'll put them on the sofa. That's what counts with art, you know.

WINIFRED

What?

LAURA

Age. The older the dearer.

WINIFRED

Do you want them sitting up?

LAURA

[*On her way to the porch.*]

No. Just put them down anyway. We can only look at one at a time.

WINIFRED

Do you know where Geoffry has got to? He went after my shawl.

LAURA

[*Turning.*]

Oh, he's in the library, making Leone cry again. Are you going in?

WINIFRED

Perhaps I'd better.

LAURA

[*Going to window.*]

Yes, do. And I wish you'd see what you could do about his cigarette, Winky. Without letting him know, of course. You say Max is in the garden?

WINIFRED

What do you mean, Laura?

LAURA

You see, he's so excited and it does take the varnish off so.

WINIFRED

What?

LAURA

It makes the varnish all shrivel up, you know.

WINIFRED

What *are* you talking about?

LAURA

Geoffry, Winky! His cigarette is going to burn the table.

WINIFRED

Oh, all right. I'll attend to it.

LAURA

[*Suddenly.*]

Oh, you haven't told me. Isn't he a dear?

WINIFRED

Geoffry?

LAURA

Max, Winky! How dull you're being. Are you sleepy?

WINIFRED

Well, how can anyone understand what you're talking about.

LAURA

Well, of course you knew I meant Max. Oh, he hasn't changed a bit. I'm simply mad about him. Aren't you?

WINIFRED

I wouldn't want to say yet. I'm just beginning to understand him.

LAURA

That's it, Winky! You've hit him right on the head. Did you ever see such reserve?

WINIFRED

Never.

LAURA

But when you know him and can see that inner fire! Oh, all evening my insides have been simply heaving. It hasn't showed, has it?

WINIFRED

Not a bit. See here, Laura, has he said anything to you yet about—your running away with him?

LAURA

Well, I haven't had a chance to see him alone yet.

[117]

But, darling, you've noticed his attitude toward me, haven't you?

WINIFRED

I thought it was reserved.

LAURA

Not reserved now, Winky. Discreet.

WINIFRED

Yes, he certainly has been discreet.

LAURA

And I like him the better for it. But I've looked up several times and caught him looking at me in a way I can only describe as—well as—discreet. Oh, I wanted to ask your advice. Would you say anything to Leone and Augustus about it?

WINIFRED

Heavens no.

LAURA

Just go, you mean? That is, if I do go. I haven't decided one way or the other yet, you know.

WINIFRED

Just go. They'll find it out for themselves.

LAURA

Perhaps it is the better way. Katherine Jewett did it that way and it was very successful.

WINIFRED

How do you think Augustus will take it?

LAURA

Oh, my dear, it will kill him.
[*She goes to windows.*]
Max! Oh, Max!

MAX

[*Off.*]
Hello?

LAURA

I've got something I want to show you if you're not too busy.

MAX

[*Off.*]
All right.

LAURA

[*Coming back.*]
Look at this one, Winky. "The Lone Wolf." Isn't he sweet?
[MAX *enters.*]

WINIFRED

Beyond words. Isn't it, Mr. Lawrence?

LAURA

Oh, Max, I've got my art collection down for us to see.

MAX

[*Ill at ease.*]
Splendid.

[119]

LAURA

Isn't this a lovely one? Of course it's just a little print.

WINIFRED

I know you'll go mad over it, Mr. Lawrence.

MAX

[*Irritated.*]

Well, I can assure you a great many people like that picture, Mrs. Mansfield.

WINIFRED

No? Really?

LAURA

Well, I should think so. You're a hard-hearted person to be able to laugh at that. Look at the poor old wolfie up there on the hill all alone. It makes me cry a little every time I look at it.

WINIFRED

He looks like Gussy.

LAURA

[*Laughing.*]

He does, doesn't he? Can't you actually hear him howling? OOOhhh—! He's probably calling for his mate.

WINIFRED

Let's see another one.

[120]

LAURA

All right. Now we have here— Oh, "Washington Crossing the Delaware." You probably know that one, Max?

MAX

Yes. Fairly well.

LAURA

I used to like it tremendously. I remember I wanted to buy two of them. One for Augustus and one for me. But Augustus didn't want his.

WINIFRED

[*Looking.*]
Here's a good one.

LAURA

Let me see.—Oh, my God!
[*She takes it from* WINIFRED *before* MAX *sees it.*]
I certainly don't know where that came from. It was never in my collection.

MAX

What is it?

LAURA

Nothing, Max. You wouldn't like it. It isn't art. It must belong to Augustus.

WINIFRED

Leone's in the library with Geoffry, Mr. Lawrence.
[*Laughing, on way to hall.*]
[121]

MAX

Oh!

LAURA

Are you waiting for her?

MAX

No— She was going to show me the garden. It doesn't matter.

WINIFRED

I'll remind her.

LAURA

Don't forget about the cigarette, will you, Winky?

WINIFRED

That's probably all over. But I'll do my best.
  [*She goes out.*]

LAURA

Poor Winky! She tries so hard to appreciate art but it's beyond her. I suppose she's been battered by the world too much. I hate to see a person battered, don't you?

MAX

  [*Sorry for her.*]
You seem to have kept up your interests.

LAURA

Oh, Max, you don't know how I've had to fight to do it. Sometimes I think if it hadn't been for my early love of art the years would have engulfed me.

[122]

MAX

You're rather isolated from things out here, I imagine. How long have you been here?

LAURA

Nine years. Augustus had to have peace and quiet. It's his liver, you know. Besides his heart, of course.

MAX

Both of them?

LAURA

Oh, yes. I'd never have buried myself for just one. I've had my share of crosses, Max.

MAX

I think you've stood up under them admirably.

LAURA

It's sweet of you to say that.
    [*With a sudden change of tone.*]
I was so charmed when your telegram came. I'd almost begun to think you'd forgotten.

MAX

Forgotten you?

LAURA

Oh, one never knows. You've been out in the world where things were happening. Oh, I've wondered many times where life had cast you. Life is so vagrant, don't you think? I mean it makes vagrants of us all.

[123]

Except those who settle down, of course. But neither you nor I were ever settlers, were we?

MAX

Sometimes I wish I were a settler.

LAURA

No, no. You're wrong. On the wing. That's what I always say. On the wing. Vagrants.

MAX

Don't you think there's a time in a man's life when he should settle down?

LAURA

Never. It's deadly. Oh, flitting from one joy to another! Art, beautiful women, charming bearded men. Not that a man has to have a beard to be charming, of course. But there's a certain romance about a beard. Do you remember that dirty old man with a beard who played the violin so exquisitely?

MAX

Where was that?

LAURA

Where? Florence, Rome, Vienna, New York— All I remember is the beard.

MAX

Was I there?

LAURA

I thought so. Perhaps not. Memory lapses.

MAX

Look here, Laura. I'm glad for this chance to be alone with you for a minute. There's something I'd like to say to you.

LAURA

Oh, my God!

[*She turns away.*]

MAX

I beg your pardon?

LAURA

Are you sure you want to say it here and—now?

MAX

I don't understand.

LAURA

I don't know why but I had always imagined it would be in a gondola.

MAX

I'm afraid that would be rather difficult.

LAURA

I just mean there's no hurry, is there? You're going to be here a week.

MAX

That's just the point. I have the feeling that I'd better be getting back to the city tomorrow.

LAURA

Max! You said at dinner—!

[125]

MAX

I know. But since then I've been thinking—

LAURA

But it's all so sudden— I've hardly got to know you again yet. What has decided you to go?

MAX

Well, frankly, Laura, I find myself in rather a peculiar position down here.

LAURA

Oh, I know, Max. I know. Don't think I haven't realized it.

MAX

Oh, Lord! Have you?

LAURA

How can one conceal such things?

MAX

Well, I hope you don't feel as though I were abusing your hospitality. I felt rather guilty about coming down here in the first place.

LAURA

Max, my dear, I'm a woman who has known the world. Do you think I would set myself up to judge another?

MAX

That's very decent of you.

LAURA

I know how you must feel about Augustus.

MAX

Augustus?

LAURA

And it's such good taste of you, Max. Such good taste. And now do you want to say what you started to?

MAX

Well, yes, I should like to. You see, if I do go back tomorrow, I wondered whether you and Leone wouldn't like to visit me some time.

LAURA

It's a very delicate way of putting it.

MAX

I put it that way because I was afraid you might think it was rather sudden on my part if I said I was —in love.

LAURA

It is sudden.

MAX

I know. But I'm really quite serious about it, Laura.

LAURA

I always knew you would be serious when the time came, Max.

[127]

MAX

Yes. So did I. I'm that sort of person, I guess. I feel I've been waiting for a long time for—

LAURA

I understand.

MAX

That's very sweet of you. And I appreciate it. And I think I could promise you we would have a very good time of it.

LAURA

Oh, I'm sure of that.

MAX

Thank you. Well, if you really feel this way about it, of course as far as I'm concerned the sooner the better.

LAURA

Oh, my God!
[*She breaks down.*]

MAX

Oh, look here, I'm sorry. I'm afraid I've been too abrupt. I know it must be hard for you.

LAURA

I was thinking of poor Augustus.

MAX

Yes, of course. I suppose I'd better speak to him too.

[128]

LAURA

Oh, no! No! He mustn't know until it's all over.

MAX

No? Well, just as you think.

LAURA

But, Max, there are so many things we must think over. You don't really feel as though you had to go in the morning, do you?

MAX

Yes, I really do. As a matter of fact, I'd rather go as soon as possible. It would be quite a lark, you know, to go up in the car tonight—

LAURA

[*Catching her breath.*]
Tonight!

MAX

It's a lovely drive.

LAURA

It would be heavenly!

MAX

Just you and—Leone and me. I want it to be quite proper.

LAURA

But Max, we would have to go without Leone. I'd insist on that.

[129]

MAX

What?

LAURA

I say, we would have to go without Leone. It's sweet of you to be so honorable. I love honor above all things. But I'm not a child any more, Max. I've grown up since you knew me.

MAX

[*Stunned.*]
Oh—! Yes— I— Oh, Good Lord!

LAURA

And although it would be heavenly to go tonight I would like a little more time. You don't feel that you have to go in the morning, do you?

MAX

Oh, yes. Yes, I really do, Laura.
[AUGUSTUS *enters from hall.*]

AUGUSTUS

Where's my nail-file?

LAURA

Oh, come in, Augustus. You're just in time. Max was thinking of leaving in the morning.

AUGUSTUS

There's a train at nine forty-two.

LAURA

Augustus! How dare you say that!

MAX

Perhaps you'd rather I left tonight?

AUGUSTUS

There's a train from Starkville at ten twenty-one.

MAX

Very well.

LAURA

Why, I've never heard! Augustus, apologize this instant.

AUGUSTUS

What for?

LAURA

Oh, you perfectly hateful man! Max, there is your answer. Wait for me in the garden. I'll come to you there.

[MAX, *without a word, goes to garden.*]

Now, Augustus Merrick, what have you to say for yourself?

AUGUSTUS

Where's my nail-file? You've taken it again.

LAURA

Do you realize you've insulted one of my oldest friends with your damned statistics?

AUGUSTUS

I left it right on my dressing table. It's gone.

[131]

LAURA

If I tell you where it is, will you apologize to him?

AUGUSTUS

Well, where is it?

LAURA

In *my* dressing table next to my Skincharm collection. Now go out there and apologize.

AUGUSTUS

[*Starting for hall.*]
I'll do nothing of the sort.

LAURA

But you promised you would. You can't go back on your word.

AUGUSTUS

I promised nothing. I never intended apologizing. I never apologize.

LAURA

You tricked me! You led me on. That's the lowest thing one human being can do to another. To trick a helpless woman. After all I've done for you. The sacrifices!

AUGUSTUS

I'm sick and tired of hearing about your sacrifices.

LAURA

Oh, you brute! I'm through with you, Augustus! This is the last straw! You'll regret it.
[*She sinks into a chair, sobbing.*]

[132]

AUGUSTUS

Umpfh!

[*He goes out.*]

[LAURA *sobs for a moment, then rises deter-
minedly and begins to fix her eyes, hair, etc.,
and starts staunchly for the garden. She pauses
to take a last look around the room. She becomes very sad, as she seems to say goodbye to
various objects in the room. She touches them
and then starts out bravely as* LEONE *enters from
the hall.* LAURA *starts back and stands looking
at her.* LEONE *has been crying. On seeing her
mother, and not* MAX, *she also starts back.*]

LAURA

[*Sadly.*]
Oh, my poor child!

LEONE

[*Startled.*]
Why do you say that?

LAURA

You look so sweet.

LEONE

Oh! Thank you.

LAURA

Leone, no matter what should ever happen, I want
you to remember that your mother always loved you
dearly.

[133]

LEONE

All right.

LAURA

In the years to come you'll understand many things
that you couldn't understand now.

LEONE

I don't think there's any doubt about that.

LAURA

My poor child!
  [LAURA *looks at her sadly and starts out.* LEONE
    *also starts out. They stop and eye each other
    suspiciously.*]

LAURA

Why don't you run in and see Geoffry?

LEONE

I've just seen him.

LAURA

Well, see him again.

LEONE

No thank you.
  [AUGUSTUS *enters filing his nails.*]

AUGUSTUS

The Holstein and her calf, by God!

LAURA

I didn't say Holstein, Augustus Merrick!

[134]

AUGUSTUS

You know perfectly well you said Holstein.

LAURA

I said Holbein.

AUGUSTUS

You've looked it up since. I know you.

[GEOFFRY *enters from hall.*]

GEOFFRY

Excuse me, but Winifred wants to know if you'll play billiards with her.

AUGUSTUS

I never play billiards with a woman.

LAURA

Well, I'm certainly interested to hear that. After the hours I've had to spend in that cold attic.

[GEOFFRY *starts out.* LAURA *stops him.*]

Now, Geoffry, I want to get this settled between you and Leone.

LEONE

Mother, don't interfere! You have no right to meddle in my affairs.

LAURA

This isn't meddling, dear; it's guiding.

LEONE

Geoffry and I have settled everything. We're not going to have anything more to do with each other.

[135]

LAURA

Just for the moment.

LEONE

[*Tearfully.*]
Forever.

LAURA

Don't be silly.

LEONE

[*Sobbing.*]
I'm not being silly. We just had it out in the library.

LAURA

[*Laughing suddenly.*]
Why, pet, that sounds like an operation. Oh, pardon me. I didn't mean to be light. What did you have out in the library?

LEONE

Geoffry isn't going to ask me. He wants a woman with more experience.

LAURA

Oh, how ridiculous! He'll ask you, pet. He may not know it but he will.

GEOFFRY

No, I won't.

AUGUSTUS

What the devil are you talking about?

[136]

LAURA

Geoffry has decided he isn't going to ask her.

AUGUSTUS

He decided that a long time ago.

LAURA

But he's decided it again. And now he says he means it.

LEONE

He does.

AUGUSTUS

I thought he meant it before.

GEOFFRY

I did.

LAURA

Isn't love involved!

GEOFFRY

It isn't love.

LEONE

If we say we don't love each other that's all there is to it. And I won't be humiliated any more.

AUGUSTUS

[*To* GEOFFRY.]
Don't you love Leone?

GEOFFRY

Not with passion.

[137]

LEONE

That's a filthy thing to say, Geoffry Cole!

GEOFFRY

It's true.

AUGUSTUS

What d'ye mean, not with passion?

LAURA

How forgetful you're getting, Augustus!

GEOFFRY

She's so young.

AUGUSTUS

So're you.

GEOFFRY

That's just it. I admire and respect Leone. But she hasn't learned passion.

LEONE

I suppose you want me to be like Winifred?

GEOFFRY

Don't be obvious.

LEONE

You're in love with her.

LAURA

Geoffry!

GEOFFRY

I'm not. I'm only infatuated with her because I'm young and she flirted with me.

[138]

LEONE

She's a nasty cat and I hate her!

GEOFFRY

Nevertheless, she has developed her passion; **you** haven't.

AUGUSTUS

But when she has you'll have her, eh?

GEOFFRY

Yes, sir.

LEONE

You think you will. That shows all you know.

LAURA

But Geoffry, passion isn't a thing one develops. Either one has it or one hasn't it.

GEOFFRY

Then if that's true, Leone hasn't it.

LEONE

That's a damned lie. I have too.

GEOFFRY

You haven't either.

LEONE

I have as much as Winifred.

GEOFFRY

Not half.

[139]

LEONE

I could get a man as easily as Winifred. Maybe easier.

GEOFFRY

That's obviously untrue.

LEONE

It is not, you conceited little pig. I could. I have.

LAURA

Leone!

LEONE

I've got Max.

LAURA

Leone! What in the world do you mean?

GEOFFRY

That's nothing. Any stupid man will take a girl who throws herself at him.

LEONE

I didn't throw myself at him. He threw himself at me.

LAURA

Oh, my God!

LEONE

I thought he was going to eat me up.

LAURA

Oh, that's Max all over. When did it happen?

[140]

LEONE

Just after you left the room. And it wasn't in fun either. He meant it.

GEOFFRY

I don't believe it.

LEONE

Yes and he asked me to be engaged to him too. There! Now will you believe it? Haven't I any passion? To make a man lose his head like that in only a few hours. You damned little snob! And I'm going to accept him too!

AUGUSTUS

Is this true?

LEONE

Of course it's true. Do you think I'd lie about it? [*She turns away, sobbing.*]

LAURA

[*To* AUGUSTUS.]
It can't be true! It can't be true!
[*She has run to the window.*]
Max! Max!
[WINIFRED *enters from hall.*]

GEOFFRY

[*To* LEONE, *gravely.*]
You're going to accept him?

[141]

LEONE

[*Seeing* WINIFRED.]
Yes, I am.   I love him.

GEOFFRY

Very well.
[GEOFFRY *starts out*.   LAURA *stops him*.]

LAURA

But it isn't true, Geoffry.   You see, it can't be true.

WINIFRED

Accept who?

LAURA

Max!   Oh, Winky, she says they're engaged.

WINIFRED

How funny!

GEOFFRY

[*Turning*.]
Goodbye.

LEONE

[*Already sorry*.]
Geoffry!

GEOFFRY

Don't try to hold me.   You've betrayed me under
my very nose.   You're faithless.

LEONE

[*Laughing*.]
I'm faithless.   That's good.

[142]

GEOFFRY

I've admired and respected and trusted you. I came down here for the express purpose of asking you to marry me. But you cheated.

LEONE

Geoffry!

AUGUSTUS

Where are you going?

GEOFFRY

To New York.

AUGUSTUS

There's a train from Starkville in twenty minutes.

WINIFRED

You're not going, Geoffry.

GEOFFRY

Nothing could make me stay.

AUGUSTUS

Albert will drive you to Starkville.

WINIFRED

I'll drive him myself.

LEONE

[*In tears, laughing.*]
Of course you will. Of course you will.

LAURA

[*Trying to explain.*]
But no one need go. No one need go.
[MAX *enters from garden.*]

MAX

Playing twenty questions again?

AUGUSTUS

Can you make the ten-twenty from Starkville?

MAX

Easily.

AUGUSTUS

I'll order the car. And have all your damned luggage packed.

WINIFRED

Gussy!

AUGUSTUS

Shut up.
[AUGUSTUS *goes out to hall.*]

MAX

What exactly has happened now?

LEONE

[*Quickly.*]
I've told them.

[144]

MAX

What have you told them?

LEONE

That you've asked me to marry you. And that I'm going to accept you.

[Pause. They all wait breathless. MAX gazes from one woman to the other. He sees that LEONE is in distress.]

MAX

Darling!

LEONE

[In a whisper.]
Oh, thank you.
[They embrace.]

WINIFRED

Congratulations, Mr. Lawrence!

GEOFFRY

Cheat!

[WINIFRED and GEOFFRY go off. LAURA sinks into a chair. MAX, seeing her, makes for the garden as rapidly as possible. LEONE runs after him.]

LEONE

Take me with you. You've got to. Please—please—

[They are off. LAURA sits staring into space, dumbly.]

[145]

LAURA

[*With a slight shudder.*]
Incest! That's what it is! Incest!

[CURTAIN]

THE VINEGAR TREE

ACT THREE

ACT III

*The porch that has been glimpsed during Acts I and
II. Wicker furniture. French windows at back,
right and left, into living room.*

*It is about 3 A. M. of the same night. The porch
is partially in darkness; partially in bright moonlight. There is no one on the porch. After a moment the lights are seen to go on somewhere inside
of the house. Then* LAURA, *in negligée, enters from
the living room. She has brought with her a hand
glass and the sketch that* MAX *made of her before
dinner. She seats herself near the light and begins
to study the sketch. She compares it with her re-
flection in the glass. She pulls her face. Pause. It
begins to depress her. She shakes her head and,
after a moment, is crying softly.* AUGUSTUS, *in dressing gown, appears in the window. He sees what
she is doing and stands looking at her. After a moment she sees him, quickly hides the sketch and
turns away, stopping her crying and rapidly fixing
her eyes. Otherwise she pays no attention to him.*

AUGUSTUS

[*With affected gruffness.*]
I can't sleep.

[149]

[*Pause. He eyes her, quickly. As she doesn't answer he comes out.*]

What are you doing out here? Don't you know it's three o'clock?

[*Pause.* LAURA *makes no sign.*]

[AUGUSTUS *gives her another quick look and stands looking out into the garden.*]

Beautiful night.

[*Pause.*]

Don't know when I've seen such a beautiful night.

[*Pause. After another quick glance at her* AU-GUSTUS *gives up conversation and seats himself. A few moments of silence.*]

LAURA

We're not speaking, Augustus.

AUGUSTUS

So I see.

[*Pause.* LAURA *can't keep still.*]

LAURA

And I guess you know why.

AUGUSTUS

Haven't the remotest idea.

LAURA

You insulted me before guests.

[150]

AUGUSTUS

Rubbish!

LAURA

I don't think it's rubbish at all! And you ordered
Max out of the house.

AUGUSTUS

Well, he hasn't gone, has he?

LAURA

Through no fault of yours. If Leone hadn't made
him take her riding and miss his train he'd have gone.
—And you said I was behaving exceedingly silly.

AUGUSTUS

So you were.

LAURA

I was not! That's a loathsome thing to say!

AUGUSTUS

You know perfectly well you've been trying to show
off in front of this fellow.

LAURA

[*Amazed.*]
Why, I've never heard anything more ridiculous!

AUGUSTUS

I've never seen anything more ridiculous.

[151]

LAURA

Oh, you awful man! Now I shall *never* speak to you again!

[*She begins to cry again. Pause.*]

[Augustus *rises and stands by her.*]

AUGUSTUS

Look here, Laura. I'm sorry if I've been offensive to you this evening.

LAURA

[*Not believing her ears.*]

Augustus! What did you say?

AUGUSTUS

Said I was sorry.

LAURA

And do you mean it? Are you really and truly sorry?

AUGUSTUS

Of course I am.

LAURA

Is that an apology?

AUGUSTUS

Yes, yes. An apology.

LAURA

[*Overcome.*]

Oh, Augustus!

[*She begins to cry, softly.*]

You can be so nice when you want to be.

[152]

AUGUSTUS

Don't cry any more.

LAURA

It's stupid of me but I can't help it. I never thought I'd live to hear you apologize to me.

AUGUSTUS

I've been nasty to you all day.

LAURA

It wasn't all your fault. I'm sure I must be a little trying at times.

AUGUSTUS

I shouldn't have let it bother me.

LAURA

Do you know, Augustus, I think I may have been behaving a little silly.

AUGUSTUS

Nonsense.

LAURA

Yes, I have. And I think perhaps I was trying to show off a trifle, too.

AUGUSTUS

Never mind.

LAURA

Some time I'll tell you why.

[153]

AUGUSTUS

All right.—Now let me see it.

LAURA

See what?

AUGUSTUS

Whatever you hid when I came out.

LAURA

Oh, that was just the little picture that Max made of me.

AUGUSTUS

I want to look at it.

LAURA

I should say not. It's hateful.

AUGUSTUS

Nonsense! Let me see it, I say.

[*He takes it. A pause. He studies it as though for the first time.* LAURA *watches, anxiously.*]

LAURA

I'm ugly and old.

AUGUSTUS

This isn't you.

LAURA

Oh, yes it is. It's me all right. Look how my cheeks sag.

AUGUSTUS

That's what made me think it wasn't you.

[154]

LAURA

[*Radiant.*]

Oh, Augustus, you know my cheeks sag!

AUGUSTUS

Just enough for character. You don't want cheeks
that stick out like balloons, do you?

LAURA

[*Doubtfully.*]

No.

AUGUSTUS

Of course not. That fellow can't draw.

LAURA

Oh, yes, he can. He's a very famous painter.

AUGUSTUS

But he can't draw. Look at that squint. Your eyes
don't squint.

LAURA

Don't they?

AUGUSTUS

I give you my word.

LAURA

You're not just fooling me?

AUGUSTUS

Not a bit of it. You can see for yourself.

[LAURA *looks carefully into the glass.*]

[155]

LAURA

Perhaps he exaggerated a bit.

AUGUSTUS

No doubt about it.

LAURA

I've always thought my eyes were one of my best features.

AUGUSTUS

They are. They are. Bosh! It's no good. Doesn't look anything like you.

[*He tears it up.*]

LAURA

[*Quite overcome.*]

Kiss me, Augustus.

AUGUSTUS

Don't be silly.

LAURA

It wouldn't be silly in the least.

[AUGUSTUS, *after a moment, kisses her brusquely.*]

AUGUSTUS

Why didn't you stay in bed?

LAURA

I couldn't sleep until I heard Leone come in. And then every time I dozed off I'd hear you snore—

AUGUSTUS
[Indignantly.]
What d'ye mean snore! I haven't closed my eyes once.

LAURA
I don't know what that funny noise was then.

AUGUSTUS
It's a cricket. D'ye know, Laura, there's a cricket up in that room.

LAURA
[Giggling.]
Oh, how could a cricket get up there?

AUGUSTUS
I don't know, but he's there. He's having the very devil of a time rubbing his hind legs together.
[He chuckles.]

LAURA
[Delighted.]
Oh, you nasty thing! What do you mean he's rubbing his hind legs together?

AUGUSTUS
That's the way they make that noise. Didn't you know that?

LAURA
[Roaring with laughter.]
Oh, you awful liar! Fancy a cricket's making that

tremendous noise with two little legs no bigger than pins. Can't you just see him?

AUGUSTUS

How do they do it then?

LAURA

With their little throats, of course.

AUGUSTUS
[*Roaring with laughter.*]
Ho—ho! They rub their legs together.

LAURA

Oh, I don't doubt that! They probably do—but—

AUGUSTUS

And that's the way they make that noise—
[*They are both laughing.*]
[WINIFRED *enters from garden.*]

WINIFRED

Well, you up too?
[*They both jump.*]

LAURA

Oh! Oh, my God, Winky, how you frightened me! You ought to know better. I knew of a woman who got a shock like that once and it killed her baby.

[158]

WINIFRED

Extraordinary! How do you account for it?

LAURA

Oh, babies are very delicate at that stage. Where have you been? I thought you were in bed.

WINIFRED

No. I've been out in the garden talking to Mr. Lawrence.

AUGUSTUS

Why the devil don't you let him go to bed?

WINIFRED

I'm not keeping him up. He's putting his bags in the car.

LAURA

What do you mean? He isn't going now, is he?

WINIFRED

Yes. As soon as Leone comes down. She's in her room—packing.

AUGUSTUS

Packing? What the devil d'ye mean?

LAURA

Winky! Has anything happened?

WINIFRED

Something's about to happen and I don't think it's going to be easy to stop it. They're planning to start

[159]

for New York at once in Leone's car and be married in the morning.

LAURA

Oh, my God, what can we do?

AUGUSTUS

Where's that fellow?

WINIFRED

Now bullying won't help, Augustus. You've kicked Mr. Lawrence out twice already, remember.

AUGUSTUS

I'll kick him out again.

LAURA

I knew something like this would happen to Leone sooner or later. She's so mulish. Even as a child she always had to have her oatmeal so dry. Do you remember, Augustus?

WINIFRED

I think you can stop her.

LAURA

I? How?

WINIFRED

[*Meaningfully.*]
Tell her.

LAURA

[*Softly.*]
Tell her—what?

[160]

WINIFRED

Tell her just what it means to marry a man that is much older than herself. Tell her the regrets you have.

[*Pause.* LAURA *is silent.* AUGUSTUS *stares out into the garden, without moving.*]

LAURA

I have no regrets.

AUGUSTUS

Of course you have.

LAURA

None, Augustus. I swear it on the table.

AUGUSTUS

You must tell her.

LAURA

But I have something to say to Max. Would you ask him to come in, Winky?

WINIFRED

Yes, of course.

[WINIFRED *goes to garden.*]

AUGUSTUS

Look here, Laura, you don't think Leone's seriously considering marrying that chap?

LAURA

Oh, Augustus, I'm afraid she is. It's positively immoral.

[161]

AUGUSTUS

It's not immoral. It's just foolish.

LAURA

You can take my word for it it's immoral as well as foolish. Of course it's foolish too.

AUGUSTUS

But this painter fellow wouldn't be such a fool as to marry her.

LAURA

Oh, he's willing. He adores her. He admitted it to me this afternoon. He asked me if she could visit him in the city.

AUGUSTUS

He did?

LAURA

Oh, it was to be quite proper. I was to come along as—as chaperone.

[MAX *enters from garden.*]

MAX

Good evening.

AUGUSTUS

What d'ye mean by coming down here and making love to everyone?

MAX

I haven't.

AUGUSTUS

Don't you know Leone is just doing this to spite that young idiot?

MAX

No. We've been talking that over for hours. She doesn't love this Cole. And I want to tell you, Mr. Merrick, that incredible as it may seem to you I love Leone and I intend to do all in my power to make her happy.

AUGUSTUS

She doesn't love you. She'll never make you happy.

MAX

That's my risk, of course.

AUGUSTUS

You're a damned fool, if I may say so.

MAX

Then there seems nothing more to be said.

AUGUSTUS

[*To* LAURA.]
Is there any of that duck left?

LAURA

In the ice-box.

AUGUSTUS

[*To* MAX.]
Care for some duck?

[163]

MAX

I think not. Thank you.

AUGUSTUS

Don't mention it.
[*He goes into house.*]

MAX

Mrs. Mansfield said you wanted to see me.

LAURA

Max, Max, how can you do this thing?

MAX

Are you so opposed to it as all that?

LAURA

Opposed to it? I could die of shame.

MAX

I don't see anything shameful in it.

LAURA

It is so shameful it cries out to high heaven!

MAX

Oh look here, we're going to be married all right,
you know.

LAURA

Married! Shame and more shame. Listen to me,
Max. I've made up my mind. If you don't drop this

[164]

at once I shall tell Leone everything that ever happened between us.

MAX

Between us? I don't understand.

LAURA

Don't pretend that you've forgotten. No matter how much you'd like to forget you can never change that—that *fact*.

MAX

I give you my word, Laura, I haven't the faintest idea of what you mean.

LAURA

There are times, Max, when a mother is not a woman but a mother. This is one of those times. Can you imagine how I feel! You and Leone!

MAX

[*Bewildered.*]
I should think the fact that we used to know each other would be in my favor.

LAURA

In your favor! Oh!

MAX

I'm at a loss—
[*Pause.* LAURA *suddenly changes her tone.*]

LAURA

You haven't really forgotten—that afternoon?

[165]

MAX

I'm afraid so.

LAURA

And I remember it as though it were yesterday! The beauty of it has never left me all these years!

MAX

Good Lord, you don't think there was ever anything—anything *serious* between us?

LAURA

Serious? That's a thing a woman like me considers serious. You see, there haven't been so many with me.

MAX

Oh, look here, Laura. You must be dead wrong.

LAURA

You deny me!

MAX

Not at all. But, well, we were just youngsters, you know— Casual acquaintances you might say.

LAURA

So that's what you call casual acquaintance! I wonder what the word intimacy means for you.

MAX

Where did all this take place?

[166]

LAURA

Time, place—what are they as regards love?

MAX

But, Laura. I assure you there was never—

LAURA

Don't protest. You may have forgotten. Honestly forgotten.

[*With a little smile.*]

I'd like to think so, Max. Like to explain your attitude that way.

MAX

I don't know what to say.

LAURA

There's nothing more to say.

MAX

No. Oh, Good Lord!

[*He turns to go out and meets* LEONE *who has just come out from the house.*]

LEONE

[*To* LAURA.]

They've told you?

LAURA

Yes. They've told me.

[167]

LEONE

Well, I don't want you to think we intended going
without letting you know where we were. I left a
note on my bed. I thought you were asleep and
wouldn't know until morning.

LAURA

I probably wouldn't have but there's a cricket in my
room. And they make such a racket, you know, with
their little legs.

LEONE

Yes.

LAURA

[After a moment.]
I would like to speak to Leone, Max.

MAX

Oh! I'll just get my coat.
[He goes into house.]

LEONE

I suppose you think I'm an awful fool.

LAURA

Oh, Leone, I don't know. Do you love him?

LEONE

I'm fond of him. I'll probably love him later.

LAURA

What makes you think you will?

[168]

LEONE

Well, aren't admiration and affection the basis for real love?

LAURA

Oh, pet, I know all those arguments so well. Affection is affection and love is love. They're as far apart as alpha from beta. They never come together. Max is old enough to be your father.

LEONE

Don't you think all this business of love is rather beside the point anyway?

LAURA

Beside the point! It's the point itself!

LEONE

I haven't found it so.

LAURA

My poor child!

LEONE

Oh, I suppose I love Geoffry, but it hasn't been pleasant. And— Oh, Mother, if I find it's a mistake I can easily get out of it. It isn't as though it were for a lifetime.

LAURA

You don't know what it is to be married to a man you don't love—if he loves you. If you're both in-

[169]

different it's easy; if you're both in love you can separate because your pride will give you the strength to do it; but if you're married to a man who has done everything in the world for you—you become grateful to him and sorry for him. It's a stronger bond than most women are able to break.

LEONE

But you don't understand. Max isn't like Father.

LAURA

You don't think Augustus was like he is now when I married him? He had everything, pet. Much, much more than Max. He was the most charming, graceful, agreeable person in the world. Everyone adored him. Everywhere we went we were sought after. I used to be charming too, you know. People were always laughing at me. But after awhile one grows tired of those things and what is there to fall back on. You want love, Leone.

LEONE

Perhaps I don't need love as much as some people. I'm not very emotional.

LAURA

You're not emotional? You're crying all the time.

LEONE

Well, then—passionate.

LAURA

Oh, what nonsense! You're my daughter, aren't you? Leone, I have something to tell you that I feel you should know before you do this thing.

LEONE

What is it?

LAURA

Do you remember when I came in this afternoon and saw Geoffry how I mistook him for Max? You must have thought it was very silly of me. But as Geoffry stood there so young, so handsome, so spirited he was the very picture of Max—as I have carried it within me all these years.

LEONE

You mean to say you've remembered Max ever since you knew him?

LAURA

Remembered him? Leone, the only love I have ever known in my life—was Max. Max was my lover!

LEONE

Mother!

LAURA

He was my lover!

[*Pause.* LEONE, *shocked, sits staring before her.* LAURA *rises.* MAX *enters from house;* LAURA *looks at him.*]

[171]

He doesn't seem to remember it—but he was!
[LAURA *goes into house.*]

LEONE

Why didn't you tell me?

MAX

Because I'm sure it isn't true.

LEONE

You mean she lied to me?

MAX

No. I think she believes it.

LEONE

It doesn't seem possible.

MAX

I'm sorry.

LEONE

Oh, I didn't mean that. Strangely enough I believe you. You're terribly right about most things, aren't you?

MAX

I'm honest about most things.

LEONE

Shall we go?

[172]

MAX

I'm ready.

LEONE

All right.

[GEOFFRY *enters from garden. He is dirty and tired. He sinks into a chair.*]

Geoffry! Oh, my God, Geoffry, what's the matter?

GEOFFRY

Nothing. I'm tired, that's all.

LEONE

[*Running to him.*]

Are you hurt? Geoffry! Darling!

GEOFFRY

I'm tired, I say. I've been walking for hours.

[WINIFRED *enters from garden and stands watching them.*]

LEONE

Where have you been? Oh, Geoffry, I thought you'd gone.

GEOFFRY

They kicked me off the train. You knew I only had fifty cents.

LEONE

[*Petting him.*]

Oh, Geoffry!

[173]

GEOFFRY

I had to walk all the way back.

LEONE

Way from Starkville?

GEOFFRY

Starkville, my foot! From Bloomingdale, five miles past Starkville.

LEONE

Oh, Geoffry!

GEOFFRY

Don't cry.

LEONE

Oh, my God, Geoffry, I thought you'd gone!

GEOFFRY

Oh, please don't cry.
   [*He grabs her suddenly in his arms. Pause. They hold each other, oblivious to everything.*]

MAX

Leone.

LEONE

   [*Coming back.*]
Oh!

MAX

Why don't you two go? In the car?

[174]

LEONE

What?

GEOFFRY

What car?

LEONE

[*Excited.*]

Mine. Oh, Geoffry, we could! It would be wonderful.

GEOFFRY

You mean get married?

LEONE

If you want to.

GEOFFRY

Where'd we go?

LEONE

New York. Anywhere. What difference does it make?

GEOFFRY

It's a damn fine night.

LEONE

Shall we?

GEOFFRY

Come on.

LEONE

Wait. I'll get my bag.

[175]

GEOFFRY

Is your bag all ready?

LEONE

Yes. I was going to—
  [*She remembers* MAX *again.*]
Oh, Max!

MAX

Hurry up or they'll catch you. Run for it.

LEONE

Goodbye.

MAX

Goodbye.

LEONE

Come on, Geoffry.

GEOFFRY

  [*As they go out.*]
Have you got any money?

LEONE

Loads. Who the devil cares anyway?

GEOFFRY

I do.
  [*They are off.* MAX *stands looking after them.*]

WINIFRED

How noble!

[176]

MAX

Yes. I think I'll take a stroll in the garden before I go to bed.

WINIFRED

Yes, do. You'll sleep better. Take this with you.
[*She holds out a high-ball to him as he passes her.*]

MAX

No, thanks.

WINIFRED

Might help.

MAX

Oh! Thanks!
[*He takes it. The car is heard. It grows gradually louder.* MAX *goes into the garden as* LAURA *is heard in the room.*]

LAURA

I knew it! I knew it from the first. They've gone.
[LAURA *and* AUGUSTUS *enter from house.*]
They've gone.

WINIFRED

She's gone with Geoffry.

LAURA

Geoffry!

WINIFRED

He just came back.

[177]

AUGUSTUS

D'ye mean it?

WINIFRED

Mr. Lawrence is in the garden.

LAURA

Oh, the poor man! Is he frightfully cut up, Winky?

WINIFRED

He'll get over it. Goodnight. I think I'll go out there for awhile.

[WINIFRED *goes off.*]

AUGUSTUS

Poor devil! He tried to get away from her, you know.

[LAURA, *concerned with her own affairs, pays no attention.*]

LAURA

I feel tonight as though I'd like to tell you something, Augustus.

AUGUSTUS

What?

LAURA

Do you remember— Oh, years ago, of course; before we were married—a young man I used to go with?

AUGUSTUS

You knew many young men.

[178]

LAURA

You probably won't remember.

AUGUSTUS

Nonsense. I always remember. Which one was it?

LAURA

He came up to see me once when you were there. He was young and very energetic. It was just before we were married that you met him.

AUGUSTUS

When you lived on 16th Street?

LAURA

Yes. Do you remember?

AUGUSTUS

Of course I do.

LAURA

I was very much in love with that young man, Augustus.

AUGUSTUS

Were you, Laura?

LAURA

Well, that man—was Max Lawrence!
    [*Pause.*]

AUGUSTUS

Nonsense!

LAURA

Oh, yes it was, Augustus.

AUGUSTUS

Nonsense, I say. Let me see. His name was Lawrence—Lawrence something— He was a pianist.

LAURA

Oh, my God! Augustus! It was Lawrence Mack!

AUGUSTUS

Lawrence Mack. That's right.

LAURA

[*Laughing suddenly.*]
And I thought— Oh, Augustus, aren't I a fool?
[*They are both laughing.*]

[CURTAIN]